Seeking an Alliance

Seeking an Alliance

A Psychiatrist's Guide to the Indian Matrimonial Process in America

Chandran Kalyanam, MD

iUniverse, Inc.
New York Lincoln Shanghai

Seeking an Alliance
A Psychiatrist's Guide to the Indian Matrimonial Process in America

iUniverse, Inc.

For information address:
iUniverse, Inc.
2021 Pine Lake Road, Suite 100
Lincoln, NE 68512
www.iuniverse.com

ISBN: 0-595-31384-1

Printed in the United States of America

To my family.
Without their love and devotion, none of this would have been possible.

Contents

Acknowledgements xv

Preface on Terms and Usage xvii

Glossary xix

Introduction or How the Veterans Affairs Administration
Contributed to My Eventual Candidacy xxiii

Chapter 1   History, Marriages between Juvenile Strangers
in India and the Diaspora 1

History of the Indian Community in the U.S. 2

Settlement Patterns 3

Chapter 2   The Dilemma: A Foot in Two Worlds 6

Exogamy: Two Models 8

Personal Musings 10

Chapter 3   Introspection: I Think, Therefore I "Om" 12

Legitimacy of Requirements 13

Ethnic Introspection: Yes, No, and Maybe 13

    Lack of Identity 14

    The Process Itself 14

    Parental Influence...................................14

    Hidden Boyfriend or Girlfriend 14

    Homosexuality..15

Courage and Cowardice 16

Holding Ground, if Definitely Against
Indian Endogamy 17

Uncertainty about the Barriers to Indian Endogamy 18

Chapter 4   An Overview of the Indian Matrimonial Process 19
              Deliberate 19
              Self and Others 20
              How "Indian" Are You? 20
              Going Native 21
              Going Native: Desperation or Force 22
              Going Native: The Ugly Side 22
              Going International 23
              Immigration Status 23
              F1/M Visas 24
              H1B Visas 24
              J1 Visas 24

Chapter 5   The Daisy Chain: Referrals at the Parental Level 26
              History and Present 26
              Cults and Word of Mouth 26
              Role of Introductions 27
              Informal Matchmakers and Their Roles 27
              Matchmaker's Appropriate Role 29
              Case Example 31
              Direct Nominations without a Matchmaker 32
              In Your Own Backyard and Questionable Sources 32
              Clarity, Preferences, and Requirements 33

Chapter 6   Help Wanted: Matrimonial Advertisements
              and Newspaper Classifieds 34
              Age 35
              Height 35
              Religion 35
              Indian Region and Community of Origin 35
              Any Indian Language(s) Spoken 36
              Who is Doing the Seeking? 36
              Marital Status 37

	Star	37
	Personal Attributes	37
	Appearance	37
	Personality	38
	Interests	38
	What Kind of Person is Sought?	38
	How to Contact the Advertiser	38
	Other Databases Linked with Newsletters	39
Chapter 7	Venturing on One's Own and Referrals from Peers	40
	Parental Approach and Peer Approach in the U.S.	41
	Word of Mouth	41
	Social Organizations in the Indian Community	42
	Professional Organizations	43
	Indian Mixers, Nightclubs, and Safety	43
	Indian Bars	45
Chapter 8	The Internet: Prose, Cons and Warnings	46
	Chat Rooms	47
	Indian Chat Rooms	47
	General Websites for Singles	47
	Indian Matrimonial Websites	48
	Serial or Simultaneous Approaches	48
	Do's and Don'ts in Responding to a Listing	49
	Do's and Don'ts in Submitting a Listing of Yourself	50
	Internet and Sense of Responsibility	52
	General Caution about Cyberdating	52
	Specific Cautions about Cyberdating	53
	Structure, No Structure, and Investigative Services	55
Chapter 9	Making Contact at the Parental Level: Telephone Calls and Dossiers	57
	Crucial Requirements and Preliminary Contacts with Anyone Anywhere	57

The Telephone 58

Standard Mail and e-mail 59

Dossiers 59

Cover letter 60

Pointers on Cover Letters 60

Standard Mail versus e-mail 62

Biodata, Résumé, or CV 62

Horoscope 62

Photographs 63

Recommendations about Photographs 64

Chapter 10   Behaving Yourself: Responding at the Peer Level,
Telephone Calls, and Etiquette 67

First Things First 67

Daisy Chain and Transitioning 67

Telephone Manners, The $64-million question,
and Second Phone Calls 69

Chapter 11   Establishing Contact: Family Gatherings and
Ensemble Meetings 73

Backdrop, The Present, and Ensemble Meetings 73

Sambandhigal Only 74

Ensemble Meetings: Pro and Con 75

Flexibility in Individual versus Family 75

East versus West: Character and Timing 76

Atmospheric Conditions 77

Where and How 77

House Gifts 78

Other Orthodoxy 78

The Flow of Conversation 78

False Advertising 79

Outcomes of the Ensemble Meeting:
Positive and Fair 80

Follow-up and Closure 80

Chapter 12 The First Date: Ideas and Etiquette 81
Long Distance 81
Driving Distance 82
Safety 82
Neutral Territory 82
Get a Room or Two 83
Case Study and Lessons Learned 83
"First Date" Defined 85
When 85
What 85
How 85
Where and Interferences 86
Preparation and Meeting Up 87
Phone Numbers and Cell Phones 87
The Date Itself 88
Dining Etiquette 88
The Bill 89
Chapter 13 Evolving a Relationship 90
Making Time to Date 90
Playing Games with Calling 91
Temporary Situation 91
Lack of Interest 92
Personality 92
Second and Subsequent Dates 93
Boundaries 94
Type of Residence 94
Introduction to Friends 95
Contacts with Family 96
Premarital Sex 96
Ulterior Question 96

Chapter 14   Rejections and Break-ups: Tactful, Tactless, Reasonable,
             and Unreasonable 97
             Decency 97
             Overview of Attraction 98
             Grounds for Rejection: No Attraction 98
             Grounds for Rejection: Different Priorities 99
             Grounds for Rejection: Geography 99
             Grounds for Rejection: Kids 100
             Grounds for Rejection: Fading 101
             Grounds for Rejection: Dossier Only 102
             Wording of the Rejection Letter 102
             Grounds for Rejection: Gut Feeling or Inner Voice 103
             Grounds for Rejection: Violence 104
             Grounds for Rejection: Deceit 104
             Time Course 105
             "Farewell," Not "So Long" 105
             Means of Breaking-up and Technology 107
             Means of Breaking-up and the Type of Relationship 107
             Inertia versus Courage to Stop 107
             Second Chance 108

Chapter 15   Engagements and Marriage 109
             Timeframe 109
             Ready for Marriage 109
             Proposals: Powerlessness, Commitments,
             and Ultimata 110
             When You Know… 111
             Proposals: Gentleman-like Behavior and Protocol 111
             Boy's Perspective versus Girl's in Proposal 112
             Rings and Other Symbols 112
             Angle for Proposal 113
             Interval between Engagement and Marriage 113

Engagement Ceremonies 114
Location of Wedding: U.S. versus India 115
Invitations: Wording 115
Printers of Invitations 116
The Guest List 117
Chapter 16 Summary and Conclusions 119
Bibliography 123
Internet Sources 125
Appendix 1 Telephone Questionnaire 127
Appendix 2 Alphabeltical List of Indian Matrimonial Websites 129
Appendix 3 List of Websites Services 137
Appendix 4 List of Websites by Community 139

Acknowledgements

I am the sole author of this book only in its outward appearance. I would like to thank my wife, my natal and conjugal families for their ongoing support and tolerance throughout this endeavor. They contributed to the book and read serial versions of the manuscript.

A circle of other fine individuals has blessed my life. Only my friend Kamaldeep Momi is listed by his name. I am indebted to him for his early counsel when I lacked experience in the Indian matrimonial process. I am grateful for the contributions provided by David Jebram, Saifuddin and Robin Mama, Prem Rabindranauth, and Mary Zaky.

My team of friendly readers included my wife, parents, sister, and parents-in-law as well as the following friends: Margaret Carr, Jane Fenicle, Susan Grimes, Cliff Newman, Lizann Schloff, Gowri Sosale, and Roy Stefanik. In particular, Satish Raj provided an astute and detailed critique. Thomas Wise, R. Viswanathan, and the Hattikudurs deserve particular citation for their kindness. José Afonso, Murali Bashyam, and Robert Kohn furnished expert assistance in their fields. Scott Haltzman has endorsed my persistence.

Vineeth John has been a dedicated colleague and friend whose infectious enthusiasm and decency have benefited me in multiple ways. I admire Peter Murphy's artistic creativity and his contributions. I thank Sharmin Hakim for her cyber-expertise and esthetics. I also appreciate Erik Grow's willingness to field my computer-based questions.

This book would have remained only an idea or entirely theoretical if Maya Kaimal and Guy Lawson did not help focus and demystify the world of publishing for me. Their recommendations supplemented their general advice and encouragement.

In the production of the book, I thank Janet Noddings for her prompt attention and forbearance. I also value Richard Bascobert's keen eye for detail that greatly enhanced the final version of the book.

Preface on Terms and Usage

In this book, the term "Indian" is used to describe three groups: (1) people who live in India; (2) those raised in India; and (3) those with ethnic roots in India. Terms such as "Indo-American" or "Indian origin" may be applicable at times, but potentially burdensome.

Although the actual definitions and usage of "Indian" may vary, I hope that the context will clarify the particular meaning. When applicable, some qualifiers may be added (e.g., "the Indian community in the U.S.").

In this book, "Indian" could often be substituted for "Sri Lankan," "Pakistani," "Bangladeshi," and so on. Of course, regional differences exist, but the dynamics are often similar. As with "Indian" mentioned above, multiple meanings also exist for these other terms. However, I am using only "Indian" for ease of discussion and ask that people with connections in other portions of the Indian subcontinent make an internal conversion of the term to suit themselves.

In this book, I discuss the Indian community in the United States, and much of the discussion also applies to the Indian community in Canada. I ask my Canadian neighbors to expand their reading of these words to include themselves when applicable, modify when necessary, and ignore when irrelevant. This is yet another narrow-minded exclusion perpetrated by a resident south of the border. Similarly, much of this discussion also applies to the Indian community in the Occident (e.g., Britain, Australia, and New Zealand). Similar modifications are in order for those readers.

While the Bibliography contains a detailed list of all the citations, the main findings of each publication are provided within the text itself. The format is the author's last name followed by the year of publication (e.g., Chandrasekhar (1982)). If there is interest, the reader can return to the original sources.

Glossary

Auntie. In Indian culture, addressing an elder only by first name is impolite. Although there may be no direct relation, first name plus "Auntie" (e.g., "Saraswathi Auntie") is a more respectful address for any Indian female elder. In this book, "Auntie" refers generically to an Indian woman in a parental generation. See also *Uncle.*

Boundary (see also *Limit*). As a clinical concept in psychotherapy, a *boundary* is an appropriate and defined role. For example, professional boundaries are maintained when a psychiatrist sees a patient only for psychotherapy in an office. The boundary would be violated if the psychiatrist intentionally abandons the usual appointments to meet the patient for tennis. The boundary would remain in tact if the psychiatrist never plans to meet the patient on the tennis court.

In this book, the concept of *boundary* is applied to appropriate and defined roles outside of psychiatry. For example, a father maintains good boundaries if he comments to his son that his daughter-in-law seems "nice" or "attractive." The boundary would be crossed if the father's comments are more suited to crude comments with the boys at a bar.

Conjugal. As an anthropological term, this refers to the family into which a person marries. The Indian counterparts to this term are *puk-aathu* in Tamil or *sasural* in Hindi. Indira Gandhi's conjugal family is that of Feroz Gandhi. One advantage of *conjugal* over any Indian term is that it is gender-neutral. See also *Natal.*

Dossier. (Per Webster's Dictionary, acceptable pronunciations include: 'dös-yâ, 'dös-ê-â, 'dâs-yâ, 'dâs-ê-â.) Webster's defines this as "a file of papers containing a detailed report or detailed information." In this book, this term refers to a cover letter, some preliminary information and possibly a photograph sent from one eligible Indian person to another.

Dystonic. Being out of place or line. For example, a name like "Krishna Ali" would be religiously dystonic. Contrast with *syntonic.*

Endogamy and *endogamous.* As an anthropological term, *endogamy* refers to marriage within the same group. An example of endogamy is one person from Madurai marrying another person from Madurai. See also and compare *exogamy.*

Exogamy and *exogamous*. This anthropological term refers to marrying outside of a particular group (e.g., a Muslim marrying a Christian). See also and compare *endogamy*.

Going Native. In this book, this informal expression refers to a U.S.-raised Indian marrying someone who was raised in India. Although the couple may settle anywhere in the world, the central difference is that one member of the couple was raised in India, and the other was not.

Jathagam (pronounced "JAA-tha-gum"). This contains the key details of a person's birth, having implications on astrological compatibility and an auspicious time to marry. It is loosely translated into English as "horoscope." See also *muhurtham*.

Limit. In psychotherapy, a *limit* outlines what is acceptable and what is not. It is grossly similar to "drawing the line." See also *boundary*.

In this book, *limit* is applied differently. Intense parents may want their son or daughter to stay at home all weekend to be available for a particular phone call. That child would be setting a limit by indicating what hours he or she would be home to receive such a phone call.

Muhurtham (pronounced "MOO-hoor-thum")/*Muhoorth*. Defined by Apte (1970) as "a moment, period of time (auspicious or otherwise), lasting 48 minutes." In this book, this primarily refers to an auspicious time to complete some key ceremonies during a marriage.

Natal. The anthropological term for one's family of origin. It corresponds with the Tamil *purranth-aathu* and the Hindi *parivar*. Indira Gandhi's natal family is Nehru. See also *conjugal*.

Referral. An eligible, single Indian person nominated by someone else.

Sambandhi (From Tamil. Pronounced "SUM-bunn-thee) *Sambandhigal* (Plural. Pronounced "SUM-bunn-thee-gull"). This term has no direct equivalent in English. It is the term used for one set of parents linked by their child's marriage to another set of parents. One of Romeo's parents could have referred to one of Juliet's parents as sambandhi, and one of her parents could use the same term for one of his parents.

Syntonic. Being in place or in line. For example, it is culturally syntonic to wear Indian clothes to a Hindu temple.

Uncle. In Indian culture, addressing an elder only by first name is impolite. Although there may be no direct relation, first name plus "Uncle" (e.g., "Balu

Uncle") is a more respectful address for any Indian male elder. In this book, *Uncle* refers generically to an Indian man in the parental generation.

Varan. (From Tamil. Pronounced with both *a*'s short as in "ago" and a rolled *r*. This word approximates "VAR-ren."). An eligible Indian male of marriageable age. English has a number of related terms such as "suitor," "boy," "prospect," "potential mate," "would-be boyfriend," "guy," or "bloke." *Varan* is the preferred term in this book, because it lacks any chivalrous or casual connotations. See also *Varani.*

Varani. (Coined from Tamil. Pronounced with both *a*'s short as in "ago" and a rolled *r*. This word approximates "VAR-renn-nee."). For convenience in this book, this term refers to an eligible Indian female of marriageable age. Alternate terms may include "prospect," "girl," "potential mate," "would-be girlfriend," "gal," or the potentially offensive "chickee." Varani is the preferred term in this book. See also *Varan.*

In Tamil, masculine nouns end in *n*, and their female counterparts end in *i*. Thus, *samaial karan* is a male cook, and *samaial kari* is a female cook. The term *varani* was coined as a female counterpart to the standard Tamil term of *varan.*

Introduction or How the Veterans Affairs Administration Contributed to My Eventual Candidacy

For me, it all began with Kamal. I could not have predicted that one outcome in my life would have partly originated this way. Kamal and I first entered medical school in Philadelphia in the early 1990s, but the class was large enough that we did not know each other initially. For the first time in my academic life, I was not the only Indian student in class. Indeed, our class contained three Patels, but only one Jones, two Millers, and one Smith. Blending into the crowd, Kamal was simply a fellow student of Indian origin, struggling through the rigors of medical school.

The first years of our medical school consisted of lectures for the whole class of more than 200 students. The cave-like auditorium provided some anonymity before we started settling into a clique or territory to call our own. All smaller sessions, such as anatomy lab and seminars, were determined alphabetically by last name. Alphabetical proximity allowed me to know my classmates whose last names began with I through L. Indeed, that roster of names remains in my memory even now. Kamal was too far away alphabetically to be in my small session.

Later assignments were not alphabetically determined, and it was novel to become better acquainted with alphabetically distant classmates. At times, not knowing them previously seemed just fine. More often, thankfully, becoming acquainted with a pleasant and previously unknown classmate led to regretting the earlier ignorance. Such was my experience with Kamal.

In our third year, Kamal and I were on assignment in internal medicine at a Veterans Affairs (V.A.) Hospital. This hospital had features in common with its counterparts across the country. The exterior of the building loomed large with an august façade. A photograph of the President of the United States greeted us as we walked through the main door. Our service there had an inspirational quality, occasionally lost during the day-to-day rigors. Not only were we learning medicine as medical students, but we were also serving the country. It also grew less jarring for us to hear veterans three times our age address us as "Sir."

During the infrequent downtime, Kamal and I chatted about life in general and what we had in common. Both of us were born in India, and our parents moved to the United States when we were young children. Our fathers are engineers. If we were anti-American, we could have argued that the American birth of our younger siblings played a role in their zany antics. Kamal and I seemed to have a similar perception on the bicultural influences in our lives and personalities.

Despite many similarities, some demographics diverged. Kamal's family is North Indian—specifically Punjabi Sikh. My family is South Indian—specifically Tamil Hindu. The language and religion differ, but Kamal believed that he would know exactly what to expect if he attended a dinner party at my parents' house. Kamal may be a stranger to the crowd, but he would not be in a strange land. Moreover, we believed that commonality among all Indians would allow us to feel at home in any Indian household in the U.S.

In our various discussions of the future, Kamal seemed clear on what he wanted. Professionally, Kamal was interested in orthopedics and comfortable with the idea of using carpentry tools on human beings. Unlike Kamal, I was not so clear and had difficulty deciding between psychiatry and family medicine. We tried to not let our prospective choice of discipline limit our learning.

Kamal and I also considered more speculative matters such as marriage. Here also, he was clear, and I was less certain. He required that his future wife be Sikh. Punjabi was implied. Indeed, some narrow-minded Sikhs equate Punjabi with Sikh. If Kamal's future wife were not Sikh, he felt that she must be willing to convert.

Kamal also preferred to marry a physician. I wondered if marrying someone in the same profession would be boring, because both people have bought the same lies. Kamal disagreed. He countered that a similar professional background would allow closer mutual understanding. Kamal's determination was such that I would not have been surprised if he had gone to India on a brief vacation and returned married.

Less than two years after our time at the V.A. hospital, we graduated from medical school and started residency training in different cities. Owing to the hectic pace of the first year of residency, we were not in touch often. When we did reestablish contact, we talked about being freshly minted doctors and some long hours at work.

In social matters, Kamal described to me a novel circumstance: the Indian matrimonial process in the U.S. Via his parents, Kamal was introduced to available young women from a similar ethnic background. The rest was up to him and the young woman. His descriptions intrigued me greatly. In fact, the more I heard, the more I was intrigued.

I had a number of questions:

- Exactly who were these available young women?
- Did domineering parents force them into this situation?
- Were they singularly dull and unattractive?
- Were they socially maladjusted sorts who could not get a date on their own?
- What did they look like, exactly?

Kamal's response to this barrage of questions was crisp: "Let me put it this way. The last woman that I dated in this way is a former model for Saks Fifth Avenue."

My response was simply, "I need to hear no more."

With that declaration, I threw my hat in the ring.

This book is a compilation. It represents a memoir of my experience with the Indian matrimonial process in America. Totally embarrassing details and identifying personal information have been omitted. In this way, this book is in line with George Orwell's observation that no one can write a truthful autobiography. The disclosures are intended to illustrate ideas, not muckrake or provide a catharsis.

This book is also a user's manual. When I was a novice, I was fortunate in having Kamal as my advisor and informal guru. I eventually gained enough understanding of the Indian matrimonial process and how it works. Accordingly, Kamal and I became peers. Later, each of us encountered the whirlwind known as engagement and marriage.

This book attempts to portray a road map of the Indian matrimonial process. It describes some other previous journeys along this road and the necessary modifications due to more recent construction and detours. It addresses the fundamental question of whether all should travel this road in the first place. It also raises questions to entertain before departing. The current terrain and travelers are considered. Multiple avenues to the same destination are examined, as well as potentially problematic areas. Rest areas and travel tips are offered. Even those not directly interested in this trip may enjoy the scenery and travelogue. Upon reaching the destination, a retrospective view of the odyssey is offered.

And now to business.

"To live is to battle with trolls in the vaults in the heart and brain. To write, that is to sit in judgment over one's self."

Henrik Ibsen

Chapter 1

History, Marriages between Juvenile Strangers in India and the Diaspora

In Indian culture, marriage is an important rite of passage. Historically, Indian marriages have not been simply a bond between two people, but a union of their families. The actual wedding often occurred in the couple's youth and preceded their living together. Upon marriage, the young woman traditionally left her household of origin and entered the household of her husband and his family. For reasons discussed below, Indian parents carried the primary responsibility for arranging their children's marriage to appropriate mates.

Many factors contributed toward determining exactly who was and was not an appropriate mate. Any acceptable union conformed to demographic requirements, including religion, language, groupings, and subgroupings. The typical preference was to marry within a group, or *endogamy*. For example, preferred unions between Muslims were more specifically Sunni Gujarati Muslims with other Sunni Gujarati Muslims. Similarly, Syrian Keralaite Christians preferentially married Syrian Keralite Christians. Marrying outside of a group or *exogamy* was not common.

Among Hindus, caste played a further role. The Hindu system is more structured and hierarchical than any other community that uses "caste" loosely. The origins of the caste system are not clear, and the word itself is derived from the Portuguese term, *casta*. The most common meaning of *casta* is a group of living individuals distinguishable from others due to certain characteristics (Almeida Costa). A further definition of caste is a class of citizens enjoying special or particular privileges. Regardless of origin, the caste system categorized people according to their profession, social standing, and defined behavior.

Any potential marriage between two Hindus had further specifications. For example, Brahmin parents considered for their children Brahmin mates who conformed to a particular caste and subcaste. Historically and by definition, all members of a subcaste originate in a same ancestral village where everyone spoke the same language and belonged to the same caste and subcaste. In the past,

1

homogeneity was the rule. Transportation was slow such that people did not regularly settle too far away from their ancestral village. In considering marriage, only a limited number of geographically close mates qualified.

In more modern times, transportation to other parts of the state or country became increasingly easier. Buses and trains travel faster than human or oxen feet. With increasing ease, people left their ancestral villages to settle in larger cities some distance away. Nevertheless, urban dwellers commonly returned to their ancestral roots for marriage. Using the same criteria as before, the parents still initiated the search for a suitable mate for their son or daughter, but the potential mates were in a wider geographic distribution.

Closer to the current times, Indians began leaving not only their ancestral villages, but their ancestral country to settle abroad. This process accelerated during the British colonization. Some Indians settled in Britain itself, the homeland of the ruler. Indians also traveled to and settled in other countries within the British Empire. Such examples include Fiji, Singapore, South Africa, Guyana, and Trinidad. In all these countries, the populations of Indian ancestry remain evident even now.

Immigration to non-English speaking countries also occurred along colonial lines in some examples. Some Indians traveled from the former Portuguese colony of Goa to Portugal itself. As a current example, Narana Coissoró is a high-ranking Portuguese politician of Indian ancestry who previously led one of the opposition parties, Centro Democratico Social. He now chairs the newly instituted Goan Community Center in Portugal.

History of the Indian Community in the U.S.

Immigration from India to the United States is not an entirely new phenomenon. As outlined by Chandrasekhar, early documents from 1790 indicate that a "Hindoo" man visited Salem, Massachusetts (Chandrashekar, 1982; Ananth and Ananth, 1996). The Indian community initially worked and settled on various farms in the Bay Area of California since the early twentieth century.

Apart from these isolated examples, the overall number of Indian immigrants in the U.S. remained small until 1965. President Lyndon Johnson issued the Immigration Act that removed quotas on immigrants to the U.S. from some countries, including India. Accordingly, larger numbers of Indians began to immigrate to the U.S. Typically, these early immigrants were men who came to the U.S. as students. Some returned to India after their education, while others remained in the U.S. In the latest U.S. census, 1.8 million people identify their ethnicity as Indian.

Although some married couples emigrated from India to settle abroad, the situation was more diverse with such single Indian men. Some returned to India to marry. The bride was selected by his parents in advance or after his arrival. Presumably, the potential bride and her family would be clear at the outset as to where exactly the couple would live. If the couple intended to live abroad, completing paperwork immediately after marriage allowed the newly married woman to join her husband. In the U.S., this processing time used to be six months, but it is longer now.

After some single Indian men emigrated, some of them wandered from the flock and married someone outside their community of origin. The extent of the exogamy abroad varied. Some Indian couples did not align with all the traditional demographic criteria. For example, such a couple may have comprised a Kannadam-speaking Brahmin and a Hindi-speaking Non-Brahmin.

In bolder cases of exogamy, some Indian men married American women. Involving some potential delays in time, this news was relayed to their families in India who had diverse reactions. In the most extreme, the outraged parents cut all connections with their errant son. In other examples, the parents recovered from their initial surprise and, at a minimum, grew to accept their daughter-in-law. In more friendly circumstances, some parents became truly fond of their daughter-in-law whose ethnic roots differed from their own.

After these initial tales of exogamy began circulating in India, some Indian parents launched a preventive measure. Namely, some parents required their sons to marry before the departure abroad. With this, any romantic encounter outside India would be adultery, and marriage would be polygamy.

Settlement Patterns

The immigrant experience has been considered in various social sciences such as anthropology, psychology, and psychiatry. Regardless of the countries of origin and destination, there are only a few distilled categories to capture the patterns of an immigrant's evolution and psychological settlement in a new country. The limited number of such patterns may demonstrate the universal nature of human experience and spirit.

An important distinction is between acculturation and assimilation (Ekblad et al. 1998). *Acculturation* is a dynamic process involving contact between two ethnic groups such that each learns from the other. Examples of this include the introduction of the English language in India and some Indian terms entering English (e.g., catamaran, chit, guru, juggernaut, pundit, and veranda). More commonly, acculturation now refers to a minority group trying to adapt to the majority. Conversely, *assimilation* is the process by which a minority group becomes integrated into the mainstream majority.

Apart from these two broad terms, some studies have specifically considered the adjustment patterns of immigrants. An early study by Meszaros in 1961 is outlined in Table 1.

TABLE 1. Adjustment patterns of immigrants

Overaccepting	Enthusiastic, denying difficulties, and possibly rejecting a former ethnic identity.
Actively Critical	Rejects new culture, while idealizing the previous one. Feels discriminated against and clinically depressed.
Inhibited	No strong feelings about past or present. Prone to emotional withdrawal, insecurity, and fear.
Hyporeactive	Perplexed, ambivalent, and possibly embittered, lonely, and homesick. Readjusts poorly.
Hyperreactive	Prone to emotional lability and violence. Deemed at risk for psychiatric illness.

Source: Meszaros (1961)

A later study by Berry in 1976 viewed immigration as a conflict resulting in three possible outcomes. First, the *reacting* immigrant attempts to reduce the sense of conflict by retaliating against the perceived source: the new culture. Second, the *adjusting* immigrant attempts to resolve the conflict by trying to integrate the two cultures. This bicultural group has no clear counterpart in Meszaros's formulation. Third, the *withdrawing* immigrant reacts to the conflict by returning home or existing within an ethnic enclave in the new country.

The correspondence between Berry's and Meszaros's formulation is outlined in Table 2. Note that the overaccepting, inhibited, and hyporeactive groups are in a transitional state or included in one of the three categories outlined by Berry. Later studies have essentially been variations of Berry's or Meszaros's studies.

TABLE 2. Correspondence between Berry's and Meszaros's formulations

Berry	*Meszaros*
Reacting immigrant	Actively critical and hypercritical
Adjusting immigrant	(None)
Withdrawing immigrant	Actively critical

Source: Berry (1976), Meszaros (1961)

Ekblad, Kohn, and Jansson (1998) outlined some factors that determine an individual's adjustment pattern. The first factor is the immigrant's personality and attitude toward change. Immigrants open to new experiences are more likely to achieve a bicultural state. These personality traits depend entirely on the individual. A greater difference between the immigrant's country of origin and the host community also leads to a greater chance for friction or retreat into a homogeneous environment. The chance of balanced adjustment is also greater in welcoming host communities. Younger immigrants also tend to adapt more easily than older ones.

Consider the implications of these findings. Certainly, there are numerous differences between India and the U.S. Retreating into a homogenous enclave in the U.S. is possible, mostly in larger urban areas. The Indian immigration to the U.S. was largely welcome and did not face institutionalized hostility. The first major wave of immigrants came to the U.S. in their 20s and 30s, young enough to allow the chance of change.

These studies have addressed the settlement patterns in immigrants. The next chapter addresses the implications of these settlement patterns on the next generation and the implications regarding marriage.

Chapter 2

The Dilemma: A Foot in Two Worlds

No matter how well prepared Indian immigrants may have considered themselves, nothing would lessen the experience of arriving in a totally different country with a completely different set of cultural norms. In India, friends and relatives constantly come and go, making the social situation in the U.S. lonely by comparison. The American accent differs from the Indian. Americans drive on the opposite side of the road. American and British spellings diverge. In many parts of the country, the weather is completely dissimilar. Customs and expectations are totally different.

Applying the studies cited in the previous chapter, three broad groups of Indians in the U.S. exist: the unassimilated, the assimilated and the bicultural. Consider each in turn.

One set of Indians has remained traditional and perhaps insular. For the purposes of this discussion, this group will be termed *unassimilated*. This group may maintain strict religious customs, prefer to speak an Indian language at home, and eat Indian food exclusively. There is a psychological preservation of India at the time of departure. This group may yearn for the homeland and praise its educational system and the general way of life there. Directly or indirectly, the shortcomings of the U.S. are denounced. This group may cite a plan to return to India eventually. Of course, that return may or may not actually happen.

Such people may prefer to live among like-minded individuals. Although the Indian community is generally widespread, there are clusters in some American cities such as Jackson Heights in New York, Edison Township in New Jersey, Devon Avenue in Chicago, and Cerritos in southern California. At first glance, all these places resemble their mainstream American surroundings. However, closer inspection reveals that both sides of the street contain sari and jewelry stores, Indian restaurants, groceries, and travel agencies. Exiting the Garden State Parkway for Edison Township, Sitar Realty is the most visible landmark.

Especially within such Indian clusters, the children of the unassimilated could also follow a conservative mindset and practices. Particular clothes may be preferred, and religious practices observed. The actual connection to India may not be as strong, but the heart lies there or with the Indian community in the U.S.

Alternatively, the younger generation could be at odds with the conservatism and orthodoxy of the older, unassimilated group. Their parents' praise of India and all things Indian may not match their own views. Similarly, the parents' low opinion for the mainstream American culture may not match their own experience or opinion. The plan to return to India may feel like a threat.

The unassimilated group of immigrants and their children starkly contrast their counterparts at the other extreme that will be termed *assimilated*. The latter group contains immigrants from India who have entirely integrated into the American mainstream. This group may view India as a geographically and psychologically distant land. It is essentially an incidental feature of the past rather than one having any current value. Drawing little from their culture of origin, such people may consider themselves entirely American without any qualifiers (e.g., "Indo-American" or "originally from India"). This assimilated group has been called *coconut*: brown on the outside and white on the inside.

If the immigrant parents themselves have not maintained their culture of origin, they obviously do not transmit that culture to their offspring, either in a specific or general way. Monocultural offspring lack the direct and indirect education of their parents' historical and cultural background. By definition, people raised in a monocultural environment have no competing cultural influences to cause conflict.

Soon after arrival in a new land, the immigrant's tendency to assimilate may be greater. Later, such people may wish to reclaim the cultural past. Previously abandoned practices are now revived. Orthodoxy resumes. Formerly casual religious observances now become more passionate. Clipped or westernized approximations of Indian names are no longer acceptable. "Matt" returns to "Madhusudhanan."

The parents' cultural rediscovery can appear confusing or peculiar to their children who may consider it a artificial imposition. An assimilated parent reclaiming a cultural past is an act of retrieval. However, monocultural children have no ethnic culture to retrieve, and any cultural matters must be acquired. This change in cultural policy can lead to a general sense of friction or puzzlement for all parties.

Between the poles of the unassimilated and the assimilated exists a *bicultural* group. This set of immigrants has retained some aspects of their cultural heritage, comparable to the unassimilated group. However, the intensity of this preservation is not as strong. Concurrently, this bicultural group has tried to adapt to the new country, which is now considered home (La Ferla 2002). This adaptation does not involve total assimilation into the mainstream. There may be an accurate recognition that both cultures have positive and negative features. Ideally, each culture's positive features are promoted, and the negative features are minimized.

The offspring of this bicultural group has its own bicultural existence and identity. The immigrant parents have transmitted some aspects of Indian culture to their children who also have obvious American influences from their overall environment. There may be a dual existence and coexistence of the world at home and the one outside. For such people, it seems perfectly normal to have cereal for breakfast, a sandwich for lunch, and Indian food for dinner. The Hindu holiday, Deepavali, requires new clothes, and the same household exchanges gifts at Christmas.

Being in a particular situation can emphasize or deemphasize some aspects of each person's "Indian" and "American" identity. For example, a bicultural Indian may remove footwear at an Indian household, but not at an American one. The identification with both influences can change with time. Typically, the younger the age, the greater the drive to assimilate. With age, cultural interests may increase, as mentioned above.

A bicultural identity can be a positive feature as well as a source of conflict. Conflict can occur if there is a clear cultural preference on an issue. An Indian elder may scold a youth for being "too American" on one count. An American schoolyard bully may taunt a classmate for being a "foreigner." To wit, this type of conflict can lead to "confusion" that inspired the coined phrase, "American-Born Confused Desi," or *ABCD*.

Exogamy: Two Models

Features of assimilation can extend to choice of mate. A few different terms describe the marriage between people of two dissimilar backgrounds. The earlier expression of a "mixed marriage" describes a couple whose origins are not similar. This term has acquired a rather negative reputation and is now often replaced with "intermarriage" or an "intermarried couple" (e.g., a Hutu and Tutsi or a Jew and non-Jew). Certainly, awkward and wordy descriptions for the same couple also abound (e.g., "She is a Midwesterner of East European extraction, and his origins are in a different part of the world and he does not share her faith.").

As mentioned earlier, anthropologists use the word *endogamy* to describe a couple from the same background (e.g., two Hungarians). Endogamy in India will be elaborated in subsequent chapters. By contrast, *exogamy* refers to a couple with different backgrounds (e.g., a Hungarian and a Spaniard). These descriptively accurate terms will be used here. A lesser example of exogamy can be a resident of Dixie marrying a Yankee. As outrageous as that alliance may be in some circles, the exogamous couples considered below are from clearly dissimilar backgrounds.

In considering exogamous couples, two types exist. In one type, one member of the couple has a strong sense of identification with an ethnic group or heritage. If exogamous, the spouse takes on aspects of that culture directly and indirectly. That acquisition can specifically include manners, customs, language, religion, and other features.

Discussing a particular couple will demonstrate this type of exogamy. When I first met my friend Nasim, he had been married for a few years. He clearly identifies with his Indian roots and religious background. His wife Jane is a white American who converted upon marriage. How these two of dissimilar origins met and married is an interesting story. Work and perhaps fate had thrown them into a common circumstance. Despite its brevity, Nasim and Jane had a number of discussions that he described as "intense." By the end of that time, Nasim proposed marriage in practical and unromantic terms. To the outsider, such a proposal may have appeared hasty. However, Nasim's character is not reckless, and the proposal was sincere. Not replying immediately, Jane said that she would need a day to consider the offer. The next day, she asked, "How exactly do you pronounce your name again?" Before he could reply, she smiled and added, "After all, a woman should know how to pronounce her husband's name." And the rest is history.

In the course of their marriage, each has acquired something. His interest in learning has been improved by Jane's general intelligence. His wardrobe has become snazzy and smarter. Jane has become so familiar with Indian culture and customs that they are a natural part of her now. She has taken the time to learn an Indian language. Modestly, she claims that her fluency depends on her audience: the younger the audience, the greater her fluency. Western names for their children did not top their list of choices. They carefully selected meaningful names that would not be easily mangled in the U.S.

In my opinion, the success of Nasim and Jane's marriage is based in the match in personalities, interests, and cultural attitudes. Nasim clearly identifies with his roots, which he wanted to maintain in marriage. Early on, Nasim must have detected in Jane an open attitude and willingness to acquire. Of course, he has acquired via marriage, but she has acquired even more. Home for them is a nice, multicultural household in suburban America.

In the second type of exogamy, one member of the couple has only a remote sense of ethnic heritage and marries someone unconnected to that culture. Here, exogamy is not a strong departure from tradition, because that ostensibly ethnic person has had many minor and major departures already.

This type of exogamy is illustrated by a white American friend of mine, Jason. Raised by educated parents in suburbia, he attended public schools. His hometown has more ethnic diversity now than in his youth. As we became friends, Jason asked me various questions about regional differences in India, the caste system, and the coexistence of religions there.

As chance would have it, Jason later wound up working with a woman, Rani, whose general background was the same as my own: Indian parents who had settled in the U.S. That is where the similarity ended. In 1947, Rani's family in India was affected by the partition of the Indian subcontinent that led to the creation of current-day Pakistan and Bangladesh. After moving to the U.S., her parents never returned to the Indian subcontinent. The children were born and raised in a monolingual American household without a significant Indian infusion.

After gaining some knowledge of India from me, Jason was interested to learn how his colleague Rani fit into that scheme. His questions occasionally stumped her. She seemed vague on geographical or historical details of India and her extended family. Out of curiosity, Jason asked her what caste she is. Rani responded, "What's that?" Later, she learned a bit about India, but she occasionally betrayed herself (e.g., pronouncing "caste" to rhyme with "haste"). Jason and Rani's friendship turned into a relationship and eventually marriage.

From the outset, Jason and Rani differed from Nasim and Jane. In the latter case, Jane had a willingness to acquire Nasim's strongly held roots. By contrast, neither Jason nor Rani had a strong ethnic heritage for the other to acquire. Both relationships worked because at least one member was indifferent to a culture of origin.

Personal Musings

I considered my own circumstance in relation to the two models of exogamy mentioned above. On the one hand, I am not indifferent to the Indian influences and heritage in my life. On the other hand, I was not clear if returning to India on vacation to marry would work well for me. Even small decisions such as what to have for dinner can trouble me such that I could not trust myself to make a major decision quickly. Moreover, I was not comfortable with uprooting any woman from her primary environment to settle with me in a distant land. The differences in our collective histories may have been too great for me as well. For example, did her wardrobe in the 1970s feature a lot of plaid and wide collars?

I have absolutely loved my marvelous journeys abroad, but the U.S. is home for me. From preschool onward, my education has been entirely in the U.S. Having lived in the U.S. for decades, this is home for my parents as well. I had an epiphany once completing the form for the Scholastic Aptitude Test (SAT). The question asked if English is my best language. I found myself a bit surprised by answering "yes." Given my upbringing and schooling, it should not be surprising that English is my best language. However, my answer to this question struck me. If I had merely reflected on my American accent while speaking Tamil, my answer should have been more obvious earlier. It would have been even more humbling to reflect on my slow pace in reading or writing Tamil. I seemed to be more "American" than I thought at the time.

So, where did this leave me? I am too "American" to marry someone who had been raised in India. My future wife should have watched *The Brady Bunch* as I did. At the same time, I am too "Indian" to marry someone with no connection to India. Routinely buying large bags of rice should seem normal to her as well.

In considering how "Indian" I am, I came to realize that much of what I identify as Indian is more precisely Tamil and my caste. Having a more fluid order of words, Tamil is a difficult language to learn. The difference between the spoken and written Tamil is especially wide. Moreover, Tamil is spoken rapidly. Tamil-speaking parents in the U.S. often have children who cannot speak Tamil. So, how could I possibly expect my future wife to learn Tamil? For that matter, if I were completely honest with myself, how much time do I actually spend speaking Tamil anyway?

My view of being "Indian" also relates to caste. Some attitudes on behavior and certain aspects of my world-view are more specifically linked to my caste. I speak Tamil like a member of my caste, because I learned it at home from my endogamous parents. As a kid, I had occasional difficulty understanding Tamil spoken by someone outside my caste.

One is born into and dies in the same caste. Unlike Christianity, Judaism, or Islam, Hinduism does not have a clear method for conversion, because of its links to the caste system. My father has occasionally wondered if some of his radical ideas have resulted in his excommunication without his knowledge. Nevertheless, I was born into this caste, and I shall die in it as well.

In sum, Tamil can be difficult, and conversion to my caste is not possible. I was not comfortable totally letting go of these influences. At the same time, I could not imagine an exogamous relationship, demanding my wife learn conversational Tamil and a familiarity of appropriate caste-based behavior.

Having a foot in two worlds, it seemed most logical to find a mate whose feet were in similar locations.

Chapter 3

Introspection: I Think, Therefore I "Om"

Searching for the "right" mate can be helped by introspection: looking inward to determine what is important to us individually. More than 2500 years ago, Sun Tzu wrote in *The Art of War*, "If you know yourself and your enemy, you need not fear the result of a thousand battles." Dating need not be so adversarial or strenuous. However, Sun Tzu's principle emphasizes the foundation of self-realization that determines subsequent action and inaction.

Introspection allows us to determine what kind of people we are. Some introspect more easily than others. Specific areas for introspection will be considered in subsequent sections. However, everyone can take on some broad questions. For example, what does one value or not? What is important in life and not? What is negotiable and not? What is enjoyable? What is boring? Career versus family? What do we want to accomplish in life?

Introspection could be a deeply serious and isolating task, perhaps most suitably done in a remote monastery. However, this is not necessary. It does require some thought, privacy, and time. Introspection can also be furthered in the context of a trustworthy and helpful relationship that actually helps to increase self-knowledge. In fact, these qualities are present in psychotherapy. Although the focus is only one person, psychotherapy involves two people, and the goal is to improve one person's self-awareness.

Short of a formal undertaking such as psychotherapy, we can reflect on ourselves by considering our relationships with others. We *are* judged by the company that we keep. What qualities in others do we appreciate? What features in others inspire us? What qualities of ourselves are mirrored in people whom we regard well? What kind of person makes us feel most comfortable? Alternatively, what kinds of qualities in others repel us?

By extension, this clarity can help determine the qualities we would value in a mate. As mentioned earlier, my friend Nasim proposed marriage after only a short time. He knew what he did and did not value. In meeting and proposing to

Jane, Nasim detected their compatibility. With a similar sense of clarity about herself, Jane must have detected the same compatibility and accepted the proposal. Similarly, my friend Kamal also had a very short courtship before he proposed. The accuracy of everyone's introspection and judgment is demonstrated by the success of these marriages.

Well before I entered the Indian matrimonial process, I once mentioned Nasim's tale to an American friend of mine. He commented that he could easily imagine my having a similar course. This observation surprised me. My friend believed that I knew myself well enough to know what type of person I wanted to marry. Thus, it was simply a question of finding her.

I doubted my level of self-awareness, but his prediction was true. I met my future wife in April. We became engaged in August and married in October. At the time of this writing, neither of us has consulted a divorce attorney.

Legitimacy of Requirements

The introspection outlined above centers on the personal qualities that ultimately matter to a person. How legitimate and practical are these desirable qualities? Consider a 38-year-old woman who wants to marry only a left-handed man who lacks siblings. Maintaining this requirement limits her options. Most men are right-handed, and plenty have siblings. She should consider the importance and legitimacy of these requirements that limit the number of men eligible to her.

It is also valid to question the importance of possessions and material objects. Some people greatly value appearances and creature comforts. If so, their spouse should have similar ideas. At the same time, others may find it less crucial to date only people who drive flashy cars, dine at exclusive restaurants, and wear designer clothes.

Attraction is important, but beauty is in the eye of the beholder. My friend Kamal's grandmother commented that good looks are not everything. She added that even if a young woman is truly gorgeous, "What are you going to do, Tikka? Eat her?" Evidently, the question was more colorful and insightful in Punjabi.

Longingly, my wife has commented that she wished for her prince charming to arrive on a white horse, but he drove a Plymouth Neon instead.

Ethnic Introspection: Yes, No, and Maybe

Regardless of ethnicity, everyone can determine realistic and desirable qualities in a mate. Additionally, the younger Indian generation has a unique consideration: How important is it to marry another Indian? Those with a strong Indian identification may want to marry only another Indian. The answer to this question is easy for this group.

For others, endogamy may not be necessary for the following five major reasons: lack of identity, "the process" itself, parental influence, hidden boyfriend or girlfriend, or homosexuality.

Consider each reason in turn:

(1) *Lack of Identity.* Assimilated immigrants may no longer feel particularly connected with their Indian ancestry or the Indian community in the U.S. The offspring of the assimilated immigrants are even less connected. If such a person lacks Indian friends, customs, or connections, then marrying another Indian would not be an interest. In fact, such a traditional marriage would be surprising.

(2) *The Process Itself.* Everyone in the U.S. knows the Western approach of selecting one's own spouse. Even if removed from Indian culture, the younger generation outside India will likely know some couples in their parents' generation who had a traditional arranged marriage. Such couples met for the first time at the marriage itself, while love and the relationship developed after marriage. The younger generation may also know how their peers married after a few meetings or brief courtship. The original or modified structure of the Indian matrimonial process may appear disagreeable or contrived to the offspring of the assimilated group.

(3) *Parental Influence.* In the Western approach, the couple creates the relationship. As the relationship becomes serious, the prospective mate is introduced to the potential parents-in-law, and the two sets of parents usually meet each other later.

The progression in the West is the exact opposite of the Indian in which parental involvement precedes the couple's formation. This involvement demonstrates the classical notion that an Indian marriage is not simply a union of the couple, but also their families.

For those raised in the U.S., the Western approach is the norm. Parental involvement in relationships may seem too scrutinizing or off the mark (e.g., "What's wrong with that nice Indian girl?" or "He is a nice boy who call us 'Auntie' and 'Uncle.' Why don't you want to see him again?"). U.S.-raised Indians may find it odd or old fashioned to involve parents in the search for a mate. The children may determine that they can better judge the suitability of a mate.

(4) *Hidden Boyfriend or Girlfriend.* One reluctance to enter the Indian matrimonial process may be that the would-be candidate is secretly dating someone already. This hidden relationship may be maintained to avoid one main issue: perceived threat that the parents would disapprove. More orthodox

parents may object to the fundamental idea of their son or daughter dating *anyone* at all. Less strict parents do not object to dating per se, but the particular boyfriend or girlfriend. Accordingly, this objectionable relationship may be kept hidden.

This situation was described in an excerpt in *Harper's* magazine and some sources on the Internet (e.g., www.ananova.com and www.indolink.com). Aballa Yones is a Kurd who fled Saddam Hussein's Iraq and had settled in London for ten years. He suspected his 16-year-old daughter Heshu of dating an 18-year-old Lebanese Christian. On the verge of this disclosure, Heshu planned to run away, but her outraged father stabbed her repeatedly and slit her throat. He then attempted to cut his own throat and jumped from a third-floor balcony. He survived the event and wanted the court to take his life. Instead, he was sentenced to life imprisonment.

Fortunately, not all comparable situations end in murder and thwarted suicide. However, young Indians may fear their parents' intense reaction upon disclosing a potentially objectionable relationship. This fear then contributes to their remaining silent on the subject.

(5) *Homosexuality.* Sexual orientations other than complete heterosexuality are present in all cultures throughout the world. The definitions and nuances of sexual orientations obviously differ. However, that discussion is beyond the scope of this book.

There is a mistaken tendency to believe that homosexuality is somehow less common or does not exist among Indians. A few examples negate this view (Narula 2002). First, a high-ranking politician in South India, Jayalalitha, is a lesbian. The book, *Same Sex Love in India*, by Vanita and Kidwai (2001) addresses the issue of Indian homosexuality.

Homosexuality is also present in the Indian community abroad. In the U.S., the magazine *Trikone* started in 1986 as a newsletter and has turned into a fuller publication for gay South Asians. Activism is evidenced in the South Asian Lesbian and Gay Association (SALGA) and exemplified by Urvashi Vaid who served on the National Gay and Lesbian Taskforce.

Whether in India or abroad, acknowledging homosexuality and generally "coming out of the closet" are difficult, to put it mildly. Sexuality itself is not easily discussed and usually considered a taboo subject in the Indian community. Indian homosexuals face an added difficulty with the high value placed on marriage. Indian parents usually like their children to marry well, settle, and have kids of their own. Responding to this parental expectation, the son or daughter has some options. One option is to use the opportunity to come out. Another option is to bow to the parental pressure to marry. One could acknowledge the homosexuality, but never act on such feelings. Lastly, an ongoing homosexual affair or fling could occur, regardless of marital status.

The sense of conflict surrounding homosexuality and arranged marriages was portrayed in three movies. Released in 2000, *East Is East* is set in industrial Britain in the 1960s. Second, the movie *Double Happiness* from 1995 portrays an East Asian family settled in Canada and the eldest daughter's course in finding a mate. The third such movie is *My Beautiful Laundrette* (1986), also set in Britain.

Courage and Cowardice

In summary, lacking interest in the Indian matrimonial process may be due to the following barriers: lacking an Indian identity, objections to the process itself, objections to parental involvement in dating, closeted homosexuality, or an undisclosed heterosexual interest.

For the purposes of this discussion, "barrier" will be used collectively to describe these five reasons against endogamy. As implied, disclosing the barrier to endogamy may require some courage. Consider an Indian youth maintaining an officially secret relationship, because the parents may disapprove. In their ignorance, the Indian parents believe that their son or daughter is truly single and may be interested in the Indian matrimonial process. Some particular candidates may be suggested (e.g., "Gomathi Auntie called and said that she knows a nice boy for you.").

The supposedly single Indian has four choices. The first is to buy time and remain vague and evasive about proceeding with the Indian matrimonial process. An initial date is postponed indefinitely. Second, the supposedly single Indian could deny any barrier and proceed in a half-hearted way with the Indian matrimonial process. The indifference on a first date may be evident. It does not require extensive training in psychiatry to detect that a person across the table seems totally bored. This date becomes the first and only such date.

Third, the supposedly single person may agree to a date merely to "shut up" the insistent parents—at least temporarily. The barrier to proceeding may be disclosed on the date and cancel the proceedings with the particular varan or varani.

The fourth choice available to the supposedly single Indian is to come clean. The parents now hear all about the previously secret relationship or barrier. Keeping any secret is a burden. Unveiling the secret can lead to relief.

Certainly, a "secret" relationship can be maintained indefinitely. However, this cowardice becomes tiresome. In the movie, *Bhaji on the Beach*, an Indo-British young woman has a secret black boyfriend who complains of being on "constant Auntie alert." The arrival of any such female Indian elder causes them to separate physically. His complaint captures the sense of tedium about maintaining secrets.

It is tempting to believe it is somehow easier to keep the matter hushed. However, being essentially ashamed of the relationship is disrespectful toward the supposedly invisible person and both sets of parents. Fearing the impact of the disclosure does not justify prolonged secrecy and skullduggery.

Making the disclosure may require some courage in facing some potentially unpleasant consequences. In an extreme case, the parents may lash out and discontinue contact with their wayward child. Such examples are not completely rare. I know one example of Indian parents informing their exogamous son that they considered him officially dead. Reconsider the example of Aballa Yones who killed his errant daughter Heshu.

In less intense circumstances, the initial outrage fades. The parents grow to accept their child's partner. With a more harmonious outcome, I know an exogamous couple whose parents initially disapproved of the marriage. Nevertheless, the couple persevered in maintaining contact with both families. As both sets of parents recognized the excellent qualities in their offspring's spouse, the initial displeasure withdrew. Ultimately, the elders concluded that they could not have hoped for a better son-in-law or daughter-in-law.

Tolerant parents accept their children not pursuing a traditional and endogamous marriage. As a country, the American opinion on "mixed" marriages and homosexuality has changed considerably. Television may be a gage of popular opinion. Lucille Ball and Desi Arnaz in 1951 were considered to be a "mixed" couple. Such an Anglo-Latino alliance would not be considered as radical now. Consider the portrayal of homosexuality in *Three's Company* in the 1970s versus that of *Will and Grace* in the 1990s.

Holding Ground, if Definitely Against Indian Endogamy

Not everyone will respect a young Indian's lack of interest in the Indian matrimonial process. Parents of the seemingly stubborn child may not respect this decision. Indian family friends—namely "aunties" and "uncles"—may not either. Moreover, these people may not keep such thoughts private. Repeated pleading and challenges may occur (e.g., "You must meet my niece from California. You two would be perfect together."). However, no relationship should begin under such force. No matter how sincere, the pleader is not the one considering the date. If pleader would like to go on the date, something is wrong.

In one example, a young Indian woman had a secret American boyfriend who would not meet her parents' approval. Nevertheless, she submitted to their insistent demands for an Indian marriage arranged by her parents. On the intended honeymoon, she deserted her new husband at the airport and went on the trip with her original boyfriend. No sense wasting that vacation, evidently.

Facing the potential flood of comments and questions may require remaining courageous and strong, if any barriers to the Indian matrimonial process are definite and carefully considered. More than a random auntie or uncle, parents may have a fuller explanation of the barrier. However, not everyone is entitled to the same level of information. Maintaining decorum and good boundaries helps everyone.

Uncertainty about the Barriers to Indian Endogamy

The barriers listed above may not be absolute. If there is any curiosity, getting a sample of the Indian matrimonial process may be educational. It may be helpful to proceed along the lines outlined in subsequent chapters. At the same time, proceeding this way would be betrayal, if there is a committed, but closeted relationship.

Chapter 4

An Overview of the Indian Matrimonial Process

Deliberate

My parents once received a letter from an Indian uncle who nominated to me his daughter's hand in marriage. The cover letter contained some details about the family and his daughter specifically. The enclosed résumé demonstrated a clearly accomplished young lawyer. However, the numerous details on the résumé would have interested a potential employer more than a potential husband. To wit, my father asked, "What do I care whom she has prosecuted?"

Contained in this scenario and my father's indignation are two characteristics of the Indian matrimonial process: it is practical and deliberate. Certainly, chance encounters and casual contacts can turn into committed relationships. These allow charming stories to tell others (e.g., "I looked in the bookstore for R. K. Narayan, and this wondrous woman held the last copy of *Swami and Friends*. We gazed into each other's eyes as we exchanged similar views on Swami. And the rest is history.").

Unlike these romantic circumstances, historically most Indian marriages began in very structured and deliberate ways. Overall, the goal of all the work in the Indian matrimonial process still is to determine if a shared future is possible for this couple. A non-Indian friend of mine has joked that on a dinner date, the would-be Indian couple must make up their mind before the main course arrives.

If early encounters are favorable, an engagement occurs rather quickly by Western standards. If a shared future is *not* possible, typically the couple breaks up, and each starts over. Openly indefinite and casual dating is not the norm. If nothing else, most Indian parents would not tolerate such uncertainty.

Such quick decisions about relationships are more likely in two situations. First, it takes time to gain experience with the Indian matrimonial process and know the pool of available mates. Greater experience and knowledge lead to a greater chance of a quick decision about the future of a particular relationship.

Second, having greater clarity about the desired qualities in a mate corresponds to an ease in knowing when that mate has been found.

A non-Indian colleague of mine described a similar process regarding himself. Prior to residency in psychiatry, he needed some months to gather some clues that his girlfriend seemed odd or troublesome. While advancing in residency, he needed less and less time to identify these red flags. Ultimately, one date was enough to determine "no." It is unclear if residency helped him determine "yes" more quickly.

Self and Others

For the sake of discussion here, we can consider Indian at one end of a spectrum and American at the other. Within the Indian community, each person has a likely mix of qualities and influences from both cultures, as mentioned earlier. Generally, it is easier to categorize people at each end of the spectrum. We can usually predict where an auntie or an uncle is coming from. The same predictive power applies to our white American neighbor who has no connection to India.

It is not as easy to categorize the generation of Indians raised in the U.S. Around its ethnic peers, this generation confronts its relative "Indian-ness" versus "American-ness." I did not have this confrontation in large numbers until medical school. In this novel circumstance, I found myself amid some Indian classmates whose orthodoxy was readily volunteered or visible (e.g., a *hijab*, the Muslim headscarf). I certainly was not as conservative as they were. On the other end were my totally assimilated classmates. For example, one North Indian classmate of mine distorted his heritage in claiming to be "Middle Eastern." I was not as rejectionistic as he was.

In my generation, I came to realize that I felt most comfortable when my Indian peers have a similar balance of cultural influences. Alternatively, I changed my expectation in that not everyone will know as much or as little in the exact way that I do. This insight turned out to be applicable to my course with the Indian matrimonial process. I felt most comfortable when my date had a similar proportion with Indian and American influences.

Some specific questions are worth considering:

How "Indian" Are You?

There is a distinction between Indians in India and those residing abroad—so-called *Non-Resident Indians* (NRIs). The importance of that distinction is inversely proportional to strength of Indian connection: the stronger the Indian connection, the less important the distinction between Indians in the U.S. or India. The more observant gravitate toward like-minded people in both regions of the world. Frequently, more orthodox NRIs travel between India and the country where they live.

The distinction between U.S.-raised Indians and those in India is also important in considering a choice of mate. Apart from observances and knowledge obtainable in adulthood, it is impossible to recreate the informal and subtle learning of childhood. For example, those raised in the U.S. can discuss directly the role of pop culture in their upbringing. Even if American pop culture is known internationally, the discussion would not flow as freely with those raised abroad. It is one matter to exchange views (e.g., "Jethro Bodine of *The Beverly Hillbillies* always resisted Miss Hathaway. Was he gay?"). It is another matter to have a mini-tutorial for one person (e.g., "This is a story about a man named Jed..."). A similar phenomenon would occur with those raised in India discussing Indian matters with those raised abroad (e.g., "Did you see Venkat Raghavan's googly?" versus "An 'over' is six successfully bowled balls."). If a person strongly wants a shared and common history with a spouse, it is important to consider those raised in a similar background.

Going Native

The pool of available Indian mates is obviously more limited in the U.S. than India. There also may be a perception that Indians in India are somehow more virtuous and uncorrupted by the supposed evils of Western society. Although perfectly untrue, this perception may make the idea of marrying a true native of India more desirable.

A U.S.-raised Indian marrying someone raised in India can be loosely described here as *going native*. This phrase does not apply to someone raised in India who went abroad briefly and returned to marry. Such a marriage actually conforms to cultural expectations. Going *partially native* refers to a U.S.-raised Indian marrying someone who was raised in India and emigrated as an adult.

The success of going native or partially native depends entirely on the would-be couple. For some, returning to India to marry may be perfectly acceptable and a long-standing expectation. If the U.S.-raised person is sufficiently at home with Indian culture, the prospect of marrying someone raised in India may not seem peculiar at all.

My wife argues that going partially and fully native favor men. She believes that it is easier for a U.S.-raised Indian man to marry a woman who was raised in India. Conversely, she believes that it is more difficult for a U.S.-raised Indian woman to marry a man raised in India. Anthropologists have observed that cultural observance and propagation are usually up to women than men.

Going Native: Desperation or Force

Some experiences with the Indian matrimonial process in the U.S. or general dating may not be fruitful. Especially in trying circumstances, it may be tempting to consider traveling to India on vacation and get married quickly to "get it over with." However, it is crucial to consider the true motivation for this. As outlined above, a long-standing interest in going native may reflect careful individual consideration of what kind of background in a mate may be most compatible. This is very different than wanting a hasty solution for some frustration over being single.

Parental force may also play a role in going native or partially native. The parents may share their offspring's frustration about being single. In turn, this may prompt them to force their son or daughter to consider expanding the search beyond U.S.-raised Indians. There may be the encouraging comment that boys and girls from India are also "modern" these days.

I know some suitably matched couples in which one person went native and partially native. Ultimately, the comfort of going partially or fully native is up to the single person. The person may have careful and well-reasoned convictions that only a U.S.-raised or Indian-raised spouse will do. These convictions may require some loyalty. One should never "settle" when it concerns a serious matter such as marriage. Similarly, it is inexcusable to marry just to calm restless parents. Starting marriage on such a basis could be unstable.

Going Native: The Ugly Side

The stakes may be high. Often, the U.S.-raised Indian wants to continue living in the U.S. Going native will require uprooting one person from the primary place and family that he or she has known. The new home will be in a totally different country away from all these familiar features and people. Many are certainly willing to move, but not everyone appreciates the full consequences of this decision. The land of milk and honey may be actually sour and lonely.

Going native entails a hurried itinerary. Even the most insightful person would find it challenging to be convinced that this particular match is made in heaven. Only a brief time is spent on this central decision affecting the rest of his or her life. It is reasonable to ask how closely this other person has considered the consequences of leaving home.

There are some disturbing and terrible tales about going native. I know of more than one example of the following scenario. A U.S.-raised Indian, "Anand," returned to India and married "Revathi." After arriving in the U.S. for the first time, Revathi revealed to Anand that the marriage was simply a sham to reunite with Ashok, a lover who moved from India to the U.S. earlier. After divorcing Anand, Revathi and Ashok are reunited.

In an alternate cruelty, "Suresh" visited India and married "Neela" who was raised there. After Neela arrived in the U.S., Suresh proclaimed that the marriage in India was motivated merely to silence his nagging parents. In fact, he is madly in love with "Veronica," but his parents do not know about her. Perhaps the sham of a marriage could continue with the known "third wheel," but divorce is more common.

Both examples of betrayal are devastating, and the deception and cowardice are overwhelming. It would be less reprehensible if all this did not affect others. By definition, sham marriages obviously involve more than one person. In my opinion, it is inexcusable to agree to the marriage if a committed relationship already exists elsewhere or if there is no intent to remain married. No one deserves to be this type of casualty in which one person realizes a wish without guilt. Sympathetically and accurately, the description is the likes of Anand and Neela were "innocently divorced."

Going International

If the U.S.-raised Indian wants to expand the search to an international level, one option is to consider Indians who reside outside the Indian subcontinent. One obvious choice is the Indian community in Canada. Of course, there are differences between the U.S. and Canada, but no ocean separates the two countries. The amount of cultural adjustment after marriage would not be as great, obviously.

Another Western country with a prominent Indian community is Britain, the land of the former colonizer. Comparatively smaller Indian communities exist in Australia and New Zealand. Self-contained Indian communities exist in various parts of Africa (e.g., South Africa, Kenya, and Nigeria) and some smaller countries (e.g., Singapore, Fiji, Guyana, and Portugal).

Pursuing any international alliance requires considering some similar issues. Is the couple comfortable with their dissimilar environmental backgrounds? Another central issue is that one person must be willing to uproot. Determining these issues early on may avoid later confusion or trouble.

Immigration Status

If an American citizen or permanent resident marries a foreigner or "alien," the former must sponsor the spouse by applying to the U.S. Citizenship and Immigration Services (CIS), previously known as the Immigration and Naturalization Service (INS). In the 1960s, a newlywed wife could join her husband in the U.S. usually within three months. The processing time for such sponsorship has become slower. Now, the wait is six months to one year. Permanent residents of the U.S. or "green card holders" can wait three to four years for their spouse to immigrate to the U.S.

The CIS/INS used to evaluate applications for sponsorship less closely, making it easier to have a marriage of convenience or one existing only on paper. Now the CIS/INS has some procedures to confirm the relationship's validity. People who marry only to obtain permanent residence are subject to severe penalties with the immigration authorities.

Consider four types of relationships involving a permanent resident of the U.S. and a non-resident:

F1/M Visas

The F visa allows one to enter the U.S. for specific academic study or a program in language training. The M visa allows one to pursue non-academic or vocational studies in the U.S. Those on an F or M visa cannot settle in the U.S. permanently. However, marrying an American citizen or green card holder converts the F or M visa to eligibility for permanent residence.

H1B Visas

American companies can obtain an H1B visa, usually lasting up to six years, to sponsor foreign workers to professional positions in the U.S. If someone with an H1B visa marries an American citizen, sponsorship for permanent residence is possible.

J1 Visas

Valid for a fixed time, these visas are issued most often to those who seek medical training in the U.S. After training, the J1 visa stipulates two options for these doctors. First, they can leave the U.S. and reenter after three years. Second, they can petition the U.S. government to remain in the country for that three-year interim. During that interim, that physician must work in an underserved area or provide a unique medical service in the U.S. The government may grant a "J1 waiver" that will eventually allow the doctor to remain in the U.S. permanently.

Both routes are difficult. It is difficult to reenter the American medical system after three years. Gaining a J1 waiver involves a great deal of time and expense. It is necessary to interview at prospective sites, which are often in remote regions and limited in number. Requiring substantial fees, an attorney specializing in immigration is also necessary to navigate the system. In sum, it is between a rock and a hard place.

One unique feature of a J1 visa is that marrying a U.S. citizen or green card holder does *not* convert the J1 into another visa or status. The person with the J1 still must leave the U.S. for three years or obtain a J1 waiver to stay. Moreover, now that person has a spouse to consider.

Chapter 5

The Daisy Chain: Referrals at the Parental Level

History and Present

Historically in India, the search for a suitable son- or daughter-in-law was conducted entirely at the parental level. Paternalism assumed that parents know what is best for their children, but there was also a practical foundation. In yesteryear, the marriage involved minors who, by definition, are not fully capable of giving informed consent.

Since the ban on child marriages in India, parental determinations on their child's marriage were no longer absolute. Now, the eligible young adults could participate more actively in the search for a spouse. It became less common for a couple to marry without prior contact. Even if their children were older, some parents may have had the same approach.

With this historical and cultural backdrop, the Indian community in the U.S. is in a different situation. Only in extremely traditional families would parents arrange a marriage without bride and groom having some initial contact. More commonly, Indian parents in the U.S. expect at a minimum that their sons and daughters will become well-acquainted with their future mates.

Cults and Word of Mouth

Let's face it: the Indian community talks. It is perfectly common for relatives and friends to ask Indian parents if they are looking for a suitable son- or daughter-in-law. Outside the Indian community, this question may be considered too forward or inappropriate. In the Indian context, however, the view is not so negative. At times, this question is motivated by idle curiosity or a probe for gossip. In other circumstances, aunties and uncles know an eligible candidate directly or indirectly. For the purposes of this discussion, this candidate will be termed a *referral*.

Married people and cult members are interested in recruiting new members. Single people usually do not bother other single people with questions about their progress toward marriage. Of course, romantic flings and disintegrations can intrigue anyone, regardless of marital status. However, married people usually want the cult to grow and encourage single people to marry, thereby increasing membership. If milder encouragement is not sufficient, married people can assume a restless intensity in their harassing single people to consider marriage (e.g., "Meeting this gem once is all you need. I'll see you at your wedding soon.").

Even if marriage is not a true cult, it is nevertheless a network of people who know other people. The Indian community is also a network. The overlap of these two networks is obvious. A balanced and reasonable auntie known to my family commented once that she feels sorry for young Americans. Finishing secondary education, gaining employment, and becoming self-sufficient all occupy a great deal of time. Personal development and maturity continue in the third decade of life, ideally. On top of all these demands, it requires even more time to date and find a suitable mate. Recognizing all of this as a tall order, this auntie argued that the Indian system removes one responsibility from the young adult. Namely, the *parents* are obligated to find a suitable mate for their children.

Role of Introductions

For the purposes of this discussion, the Tamil term *varan* will be used to describe a young man from an Indian background who is eligible for marriage. *Varani* is a coined term for the female counterpart. It is best for parents introducing a varan or varani to their child to consider this simply as an introduction.

To repeat, it is only an introduction.

Indian parents in the U.S. may hold the responsibility of doing the groundwork in obtaining a varan or varani for their children, but the subsequent course of that potential relationship is not within their control. Of course, parental influences play a role in helping to create or destroy a relationship. However, the parents' involvement should occur only up to a point. The two members of the couple themselves must assume most of the responsibility for a relationship. That responsibility is theirs and belongs to no one else. After all, the bottom line on a marriage certificate has only two names. I hasten to add that the same is true for divorce papers.

Informal Matchmakers and Their Roles

Even outside the Indian community, the most common way that a married couple met is via friends, usually direct peers. The formality of that introduction varies. An informal circumstance may involve being at the right place at the right time, such as two people meeting and chatting at a dinner party at a mutual friend's place. A more artificial circumstance is a blind date or a set-up organized by a mutual friend.

In the Indian community, referrals occur at more levels, as discussed below. Merely by virtue of being Indian, aunties and uncles inform their friends of an available varan or varani. The single person's peers may do the same.

An overview of the parties is outlined in Figure 1. This "daisy chain" is made possible at the outset if, and only if, both boy and girl are willing and interested in proceeding.

Figure 1. Daisy Chain

Boy's Parents   ⇔   Matchmaker   ⇔   Girl's Parents
⇓   ⇓

Boy   Girl

Figure 2 demonstrates a few possible initial contacts. One set of parents can talk with someone known to them regarding a referral. Alternatively, this "matchmaker" may approach one set of parents about a referral.

Figure 2. Initial Contacts

Boy's Parents   ⇔   Matchmaker   ⇔   Girl's Parents

After the initial contacts with the matchmaker, Figure 3 illustrates the parallel discussions between parent and child. Considering the known details, the boy's side may discuss, "We spoke to Sharadha Auntie who knows a nice girl in New Jersey who studied architecture." Similarly, the girl's side may discuss, "We spoke to Sharadha Auntie who knows a nice boy in Pennsylvania who studied botany."

As discussed in greater detail in Chapter 9, the boy and girl should have interest in proceeding with the general Indian matrimonial process and this particular referral. If the boy or girl does not want to proceed, that is the end of the story. All the other figures below do not apply.

Figure 3. Preliminary Discussions

Boy's Parents   Girl's Parents
⇓   ⇓

Boy   Girl

The next step is illustrated in Figure 4A. Each set of parents informs the matchmaker about the interest in proceeding. Alternatively, the matchmaker should receive the news that the boy or girl does not want to proceed. As outlined in Figure 4B, the matchmaker relays the good or bad news from one set of parents to the other. With bad news, nothing further should occur. That is the end of the story, and Figures 5 and 6 do not apply.

Figure 4A. Parents to Matchmaker

Boy's Parents   →   Matchmaker   ←   Girl's Parents

Figure 4B. Matchmaker to Parents

Boy's Parents   ←   Matchmaker   →   Girl's Parents

Good news is another story. A mutual interest in proceeding prompts the matchmaker to assists in the exchange of the parents' telephone numbers usually. The discussion between the two sets of parents is illustrated in Figure 5.

Figure 5. Sambandhigal

Boy's Parents   ↔   Girl's Parents

There may be a decision to exchange dossiers, as outlined in a subsequent chapter. Defying direct translation into English is the useful Tamil word *sambandhi* (plural: *sambandhigal*). This term describes the relationship between two sets of parents linked by their children's marriage. Romeo's mother or father was a *sambandhi* to Juliet's mother or father and vice versa.

As demonstrated in Figure 6, the ultimate goal of all this maneuvering is the boy and girl establishing contact. The rest is up to them. It is wonderful if the relationship is proceeding well. Ideally, the couple has much in common and enjoys each other's company. A relationship should not be forced into "proceeding well" for other reasons. Parents or others can be earnest, but this should not translate into interfering with the young couple's relationship. This represents poor boundaries or a lack of appropriate roles and privacy.

Figure 6. Couple

Boy   ↔   Girl

Matchmaker's Appropriate Role

By definition, a matchmaker is in the middle and must determine if the referral is welcome or not. If one party is *not* interested for whatever reason, the matchmaker must respect such sentiments and abandon his or her own preferences and wishes. Even if this matchmaker believes that this potential match is ideal, both members of the "ideal" couple must be interested in proceeding in the first place. If both are not interested, then the matchmaker has no match to make. Again, the would-be matchmaker must respect this decision not to proceed. If there is definitely no interest, the single person may need to stand ground against a fanatical matchmaker.

It is a different story if a matchmaker is providing a welcome referral to two interested parties. In the best scenario, the matchmaker makes a selective referral based on the perceived compatibility of the potential couple. The matchmaker's role exists because both members of the couple presumably do not know each other. If the two already knew each other, the matchmaker's referral would be redundant. A ski buff entering a ski area already knows skiing is available.

As illustrated above, a series of exchanges between the matchmaker and the two parties may be appropriate at the beginning. After introductions have occurred, the matchmaker's essential task is complete. Note that the matchmaker is absent in Figures 5 and 6. The matchmaking role is purely temporary and expires quickly.

A brief word to the matchmaker at the beginning may be helpful and appropriate (e.g., "We talked on the phone and plan to meet next weekend."). An ongoing series of updates to the matchmaker is unnecessary and inappropriate. No one should feel obligated to provide such updates, and the matchmaker should not expect them.

If a referral actually proceeds well, it would be kind and gracious to thank the matchmaker with a brief statement or gesture (e.g., phone call, card, or a gift). Conversely, the matchmaker should briefly hear about the end of a relationship. The only intent is to relay news—nothing else. This is not a place for blame. This news may help avoid embarrassing questions or situations later (e.g., "What shall I wear to your wedding?").

If a relationship has not proceeded well or ended outright, do not blame the matchmaker or referring source. Do not execute the messenger. As demonstrated in Figures 1 through 4 earlier, the usually well-intentioned matchmaker took the time to do some initial groundwork in serving as an intermediary. The matchmaker cannot be held accountable for anything else (i.e., Figures 5 and 6). The matchmaker should not hear complaint that should be contained within the couple (e.g., "Why did you fix me up with that horror?"). This also represents good boundaries. That matchmaker generously thought that these two would be a good couple and made a recommendation in the first place. Turning around and blaming that matchmaker is ungrateful and misguided. If boy and girl agreed to proceed, the progression of the relationship is up to them only.

Here is a simple example. If you like pizza, it is nice of a friend to recommend a new pizza parlor that welcomes new customers. That friend may provide the telephone number and address of the pizza parlor. Assume that neither your friend nor a probation officer is forcing you to go there. Your friend need not go to the pizza parlor with you on the first or subsequent times. You need not describe in exquisite detail all the features of your experience there (e.g., when you arrived, where you parked, the special of the day, the name of the waiter, and when you left). If you enjoyed the experience, it is polite to thank your friend accordingly. You may be further grateful if this referral led to a committed relationship between the restaurant and you as the patron.

On the other hand, any unpleasant experience there may not be your friend's fault. Your friend thought that it would work out, but it did not. That's life. Giving the pizza parlor a chance may be appropriate or not. Recontacting and harassing your friend for an unsatisfying recommendation would not be polite. Similarly, you are not obligated to provide your friend repeated updates every time that you consider visiting the pizza parlor. Your friend should not seek this either. It would be misdirected to tell the chef that your friend was a fool to recommend this place.

Case Example

An example independent of food may be more illustrative. A friend of my parents, Kamini Auntie, once asked them if I would be interested in a blind date. She believed that this varani, Renuka, and I would make a good couple.

My parents received my consent to proceed, and Renuka's parents obtained hers. Kamini Auntie heard about the mutual interest and provided appropriate telephone numbers. As the interested parties, Renuka and I did the rest. The initial meeting went satisfactorily enough to justify further dates. Soon after the initial meeting, my parents encountered Kamini Auntie and briefly mentioned the initial meeting. There was not a huge discussion replete with salacious details, even if there were any. I am sure that my parents thanked Kamini Auntie. Maintaining good boundaries, that auntie did not pester my parents with questions about the initial meeting or the later course. Her role as matchmaker had expired after the first meeting between Renuka and me.

Ultimately, the relationship between Renuka and me did not work out. Kamini Auntie felt terribly sorry and directly responsible for the outcome. She even wondered if my parents and I were angry with her for making the referral in the first place. Her sympathies were kind. Her sense of responsibility, however, was excessive. She participated in an initial contact between Renuka and me.

That is all.

Kamini Auntie did not attend the initial meeting. She was not responsible for the time that we met, what we wore, discussed, or ate. By implication, we cannot hold her responsible for anything at subsequent meetings. It would have been inappropriate for Renuka or me to disclose to Kamini Auntie the full details about any misgivings in our would-be relationship. Asking Kamini Auntie to intervene would have been more inappropriate. Similarly, my parents or Renuka's parents did not disclose such misgivings to Kamini Auntie, their mutual friend. It would have been maximally inappropriate for any parent to disclose such details without Renuka's knowledge or mine.

Direct Nominations without a Matchmaker

In some circumstances, aunties and uncles can nominate their own child as the referral. In this case, the auntie or uncle is serving as the matchmaker as well as parent of the referral. If the families have known each other for some time, this recommendation can be awkward (e.g., "Your Kumar has known my daughter Uma since they were kids, and I was thinking that they would make a nice couple. What do you say?"). Social scientists and others have observed a nearly universal taboo against incest such that children raised together typically do not marry. Familiarity does breed contempt. Nevertheless, a zealous Indian parent may proceed undeterred in approaching an old family friend regarding their children pairing up. One former varani declared that she would not marry anyone who played in the same sandbox with her during childhood.

In Your Own Backyard and Questionable Sources

Despite its closeness, a local college is always a world away from home. Similarly, a local referral is worth considering, if the shared history is not lengthy. "Local" here refers to the same general region, not simply the same neighborhood. The Indian community is relatively small, and people often do know each other locally and farther afield. It may be tempting to assume that all eligible Indian candidates within a radius must be known. However, this line of thought is akin to thinking that all black people know each other. Why should all Indians know all other Indians?

My friend Kamal's parents live less than two hours away from the couple who became their sambandhigal. Both families were amazed that they had never met. In my case, my future wife and I were living 50 miles apart when we first met. It also turned out that my mother-in-law's close relative lives only an hour away from my parents' house. I know an uncle who is well-connected to the Gujarati community in his region. If he has never heard of a particular Gujarati family, he is inclined to believe that they must not exist.

Upon meeting, connecting the dots and establishing mutual Indian connections are common. When my father-in-law and my parents first met, they determined that my father's old classmate from forty years ago is distantly related to my father-in-law. Small world. In tracing other connections, my wife and I have been surprised that neither our families nor the two of us had crossed paths earlier.

Imagine a referral coming from a more questionable source. Although the person is also Indian, that person's interests and judgment may be different. After all, the same ethnicity does not guarantee homogeneity. Even if this Indian person is not considered truly a friend, an acquaintance with this person can occur with repeated encounters at Indian parties and functions. A referral from this questionable person may be considered questionable as well (i.e., it takes one to know one). Once, I discussed this issue with my parents. My father's incisive response was that *we* also know the questionable person. How dare do we cast doubt on the referrals from him or her?

Clarity, Preferences, and Requirements

Regardless of the referral's source, people should be clear on what type of person would qualify or appeal to them. For example, if the future mate must be vegetarian, not smoke and speak Hindi, a referral to a non-vegetarian, Telugu smoker would not be worthwhile structurally. Even if that person is really "nice," the dietary and linguistic requirements would create impossible barriers. As outlined in the earlier discussion on introspection, clarifying these requirements at the outset allows a clear foundation for proceeding. This type of clarity saves everyone time. This is different than approaching the Indian matrimonial process as a roll of the dice or a formless ramble.

Establishing a foundation of well-reasoned requirements may also provoke a downpour of contrary comments (e.g., "If you only met this person, you would really change your mind."). Valid challenges require reconsidering the requirements (e.g., "Why are you rejecting this varan because he has no dimples?"). However, well-considered requirements may entail holding ground.

Preferences differ from requirements entirely. For example, preferring someone speaking a particular Indian language is different than requiring this. Preferring a vegetarian mate does not disqualify non-vegetarians. Requiring a vegetarian mate *does* disqualify non-vegetarians.

Chapter 6

Help Wanted: Matrimonial Advertisements and Newspaper Classifieds

In the classifieds, there are personal advertisements in newspapers such as the *Washington Post*. Within the space of a few lines, these personal ads try to capture the attention of an interested party. Often in a lighthearted or colorful way, the ads aim to access a pool of like-minded people whom the advertiser does not know currently. Although deliberate and unromantic, these ads can be effective in connecting with someone new. At first glance, it is discouraging to see that personal ads are on the same page as real estate and merchandise for sale. A practical view is that these ads can be the origin of a committed relationship.

Typically, a newspaper has a wider appeal than a magazine such as *Harper's* or the *New York Review of Books*, which also feature personal ads. With some self-selection, two readers of the *New York Review of Books* may have more in common than two readers of a general newspaper. Personal advertisements are also found in newspapers oriented to a specific community such as the *Washington Jewish Weekly*.

For the Indian community in North America, one popular publication is *India Abroad*, which also features personal advertisements. All these advertisements attempt to establish a relationship with a like-minded person in the geographically wide distribution of the Indian community. Personal advertisements in *India Abroad* are termed, "matrimonials." The change in terminology also signals a change in outlook. Personal ads in other publications may be more casual, but Indian ads are placed with the goal of marriage.

The wording of the matrimonial ads tends to be sober and direct. Commonly listed features include the following: age, height, religion, marital status, Indian region and community of origin, any Indian language(s) spoken, and the seeker. A broader and often vague category is personal attributes. The ad may also contain information on what kind of person is sought and what is not required (i.e.,"no bars"). Lastly, the ad contains information on how to contact the person in question. The person placing the ad in *India Abroad* is not necessarily the same as the person seeking a relationship.

Consider each feature in greater detail:

Age

This feature is self-explanatory. Honesty is the rule. If important, the preferred age range in the mate is also listed. If age range is unlisted, a wide range of responses can be expected. There may be some opportunities for cradle robbing or potential intrigue in dating a more "mature" person.

Height

With the American insistence on the archaic imperial system, height is usually listed in feet and inches. A listing in centimeters typically signifies that a person is raised in India or abroad, or possibly an ambidextrous Canadian who forgot to provide an imperial conversion for their lazy neighbors to the south. Descriptive terms such as "tall" are obviously open to interpretation.

Religion

Even if the majority of the Indian population is Hindu, a caste or another group name may imply the same information. For example, "Pillai" signifies a South Indian Hindu. Ads may be more specific regarding religious designation (e.g., Syrian Christian). This information may be intended to convey roots or a requirement in a mate. A Sunni Muslim may want to marry only another Sunni Muslim. If religion is not important, the ad may state plainly "religion no bar."

Indian Region and Community of Origin

Usually, the ad provides more specific information on roots in the Indian subcontinent. Often, this overlaps with a particular language such as Gujarat and Gujarati. If the person has settled outside the original region, this information may also be specified (e.g., "Keralite raised in Delhi"). Community of origin can vary in its level of specificity. For example, "Tamil Brahmin" is at one level of specificity, but "Tamil Iyer Vadama" is more specific in conveying respectively region, caste, and subcaste. As with religion, details about region or community of origin may provide a sense of the person's history or serve as a requirement in a future mate.

Any Indian Language(s) Spoken

The parental generation in the U.S. often speaks an Indian language or two, but their children vary from the fully conversant to the unable. The less-than-fluent may face ridicule from insensitive speakers of the same language, even if they are relatives. Repeated ridicule may silence any attempt at speaking such a language.

Fluency in an Indian language may influence the kind of mate desired. In my case, I preferred a Tamil-speaking wife, partly because I wanted to continue the ability to gossip in Tamil while in public in the U.S. Most of my relatives are at least bilingual, but some older relatives speak only Tamil. Even bilingual relatives may prefer to speak Tamil rather than English. If my wife did not speak or understand Tamil, she would be excluded from such conversations. Direct exchanges with such relatives would not be possible for her.

One should identify for oneself the importance of such language-based issues. A person may feel strongly about speaking an Indian language and require this in a mate. This would help transmit that language to a subsequent generation. If so, this requirement entails seeking an appropriate person.

Certainly, it is possible to learn any language, if there is interest. A friend of mine married a woman who initially knew no Hindi. After marriage, she took the time, money, and effort to learn Hindi. Her ultimate fluency was demonstrated by her comfort in traveling across North India without her husband. They talk to their U.S.-born children in Hindi.

Not all spouses would be this dedicated to learning a new language. Learning especially an Indian language is not easy. It requires energy and commitment to find appropriate resources. Practice requires more time. It is too easy to fall back on English and not learn the Indian language. Typically, people learn another language best when there is no alternative. A Scandinavian friend of mine lived in South America for a prolonged assignment. Total immersion in Spanish forced him to learn quickly. He also informed me of the Spanish saying that, "The better dictionary has dark hair." Indeed, his comfort in Spanish greatly improved when he started dating a local chica.

If a person is not fluent in an Indian language, this requirement in a future mate may not be as appropriate. The parents may be more interested in this common linguistic background more than the child for whom that Indian language is not integral.

Who is Doing the Seeking?

Ads often list this specifically. If the parents are doing the seeking, there is a greater chance that their son or daughter is U.S.-raised (e.g., "Jain parents seek match for their U.S.-raised son."). If someone else is doing the seeking, the person may not be U.S.-raised (e.g., "Brother seeks an alliance for his sister.").

Marital Status

If unspecified, the person is presumably single. Those who are not single vary in their candor. Some specify that they are divorced while others may not. Any previous relationship that produced no children is usually termed "issueless." Some divorcés may specify that it was an "innocent divorce." Indeed, previous chapters have highlighted a few unfortunate victims of trickery that ultimately led to a justifiable divorce. If the divorce occurred for other reasons, "innocent" is usually omitted.

Star

Among Hindus, the planetary and other celestial locations at birth determine a specific designation known as *nakshathram*, loosely translated as "star." The range of these categories is more diverse than a Western zodiac. A specific nakshathram is also linked to specific predictions such as wealth or illness. Unlike the view of Western astrology, an Indian nakshathram is more mainstream, and its implications for marriage are discussed later.

Personal Attributes

This is a diffuse and highly subjective category. Crucial to any relationship, personal attributes relate to external and internal qualities. The conscientious may have difficulty determining what personal details to list in the ad and struggle to contain their modesty. Others have decreased difficulty with being boastful. Three common categories of attributes include appearance, personality, and interests.

Appearance

Ultimately, all of this is a question of accuracy in self-appraisal and modesty. Attraction and beauty do lie in the eye of the beholder. The balance is between a favorable and accurate portrayal without overstatement. In my survey of ads, references to appearance start at "beautiful," "pretty," or "handsome." Words such as "extremely" and "exceptionally" distinguish the best within the superior (e.g., "exceptionally beautiful"). Frankly, it is not clear to me if the Indian community or any other can actually contain so many stunning people.

References to complexion can enter these ads, as the Indian community stereotypically favors light skin to dark skin. "Fair" with various modifiers can be found. Less common with ads in the U.S., "wheatish" is also found. Terms such as "olive" and "alabaster" are uncommon and essentially Western descriptions.

Personality

Ads describing women often include "sweet" and "charming." Ads describing men may convey that he is basically a nice guy. The general quality and impression of the ad are probably more revealing than any particular word. Negative qualities are typically omitted. After all, why would anyone list "rude and boring" in an ad?

Ads can state that the person has a "blend of Indian and Western values" or a similar phrase. Alternatively, the ads list the person having a "respect for Indian values." These phrases seem curious to me. Categorizing a value as "Indian" or "Western" is not always possible or easy. For example, where would "hardworking" fall? Moreover, only those with a blend of such values would place or respond to such an ad in the first place. Why would anyone without "respect for Indian values" consider marriage to an Indian?

Interests

The ads may list a person's interests such as sports. The general sense is that walking to the car does not produce shortness of breath in that person. Other interests may indicate that the person has some social skills or other attributes (e.g., "outgoing personality"). Strength of religious conviction can be conveyed directly or indirectly (e.g., "God-fearing" or "traditional").

What Kind of Person is Sought?

In the Indian system, the future spouse is often known as the "match." If important, the ad may list the preferences or requirements in the match such as the following: age range, community of origin, profession, and geographical requirements. As mentioned above, the wording of the personal ad conveys the advertiser's personality. By implication, the person reading the ad can detect some compatibility or incompatibility.

How to Contact the Advertiser

After providing some or all of the information given above, the ad will list how to contact the advertiser. Placing the matrimonial ad requires giving up a variable amount of privacy. For example, the Indian population in Chicago is so sizeable that "Raj" with a general post office box could be one of many. However, Raj in

Caribou, Maine may be only one person. If his ad lists his local address, Raj's privacy may be compromised.

Solving this potential problem, *India Abroad* offers its own post boxes for listing in classified ads. The newspaper forwards all responses to the advertiser. In this circumstance, Raj in Chicago would be as anonymous as Raj in Caribou.

The issue of privacy in ads is equally relevant with telephone numbers. Telephone directories have a list of area codes and corresponding regions. As above, a telephone number in an area code with a large Indian community can be essentially anonymous. For example, there is no shortage of Indians in the 212 area code of Manhattan. On the other hand, listing a phone number in Nebraska may be more revealing.

Personal ads may list an e-mail address. Cyberspace is indeed vast, but not as vast as it may appear at first. Here also, the level of privacy can vary. Ads clearly containing a name more easily reveal identity (e.g., lakshmikumar@domain.com). Clipped names, initials, or numbers are more likely to preserve anonymity (e.g., lk101@domain.com).

Other Databases Linked with Newsletters

Smaller groups within the Indian community maintain matrimonial services and databases. Examples include the International Brahman Association (IBA) and North AMerican Ayyangar Association (NAMA). Both are linked with charities and have nominal fees for membership. Their newsletters have brief and anonymous matrimonial listings, limited to year of birth, place of residence, and height. The registrants have granted tacit permission to have more detailed information about them released to any interested party. The heads of the organizations serve as an intermediary or matchmaker as outlined in Figures 1 through 6 in Chapter 5.

Chapter 7

Venturing on One's Own and Referrals from Peers

In India historically, parents of the unmarried person received referrals, as described earlier. The parents arranged their children's marriage, not the children themselves. Children may reject or approve of a prospective mate for different reasons than adults. For example, if my sister's preadolescent suitors actually married her, she would have already been married and divorced a few times by ninth grade.

Since the ban on childhood marriages, India experienced a universal sociological phenomenon. As the general level of education among females increased, the average age of marriage increased, and the number of offspring decreased.

Considering marriage between young adults implied the possibility of the young couple being more involved in the matrimonial process. Telling a six-year old, "You are marrying this girl" could be in the same spirit as telling him to brush his teeth. Dental hygiene and marriage are different matters.

The nature of any protest against marriage is worth considering. My mother-in-law's cousin had some reservations about her marrying my father-in-law who owned at least one torn t-shirt back then. This reservation did not prevent the marriage from proceeding. More credible protests may be based on detecting warning signs. A shy person hesitating to marry an obviously domineering person may be more appropriate. It would be naïve to believe that marriage will change a lion into a meek pussycat.

With the decline of child marriages, unarranged or "love marriages" became more common in India. The specifics of actual courtship totally varied. Sometimes, the genteel proceeding was no more scandalous than a novel by Jane Austen. In other examples, the secret couple developed a powerful infatuation or lust.

A love marriage is certainly not the historical norm in India, and the disclosure can produce a sense of scandal. A love marriage within the same caste may relieve the parents, even if they did not play a role in creating that relationship. In my extended family, there are two examples of this type of love marriage. Of course, the parents may still have some uncomfortable questions. The Tamil expression carrying a negative overtone is *"ooru sutharathu"* or "going around town." Nevertheless, the parents were ultimately fine with the couple.

In other cases, revealing a romantic relationship can be more scandalous. In one example in India, a Hindu boy, "Nikil," married a Christian girl, "Susan," in a civil ceremony. Both sets of parents were stunned by this announcement, but they grew to accept the relationship. Each person accepted alternates for their actual names: "Nicholas" for "Nikil" and "Suman" for "Susan." Although the parents were welcoming, some remote relatives were openly displeased. Later, Susan disappeared without warning and never returned.

Clearly, the Indian community in the West has a different set of circumstances. Full orthodoxy can be transmitted to the next generation, but a decreased level of observance is certainly possible. Whatever the level of orthodoxy, the children simply may not fully inform their parents of their activities. For that matter, selective disclosure to parents occurs regardless of orthodoxy, culture, and race.

Parental Approach and Peer Approach in the U.S.

The previous chapter described how Indian parents in the U.S. can play a role in setting up their children with potential mates. As described below, the single person can use a few parallel venues on the same quest.

Word of Mouth

Outside the Indian community, the most common means by which a person meets a future mate is via mutual friends. The same system can apply to the Indian community. I know at least two well-matched couples that came together this way.

It may not hurt to try a date arranged by a friend. Friends who know someone well also have a sense of potentially compatible mates. Like-minded people may know other like-minded people who could be a good match.

I had one such experience. A pleasant and gentle friend of mine thought that I would be a good match for a family friend of hers who lived near me. I was flattered and called the varani. The reasonably lively phone calls were reciprocated. With time, we decided to meet directly.

Anticipating our first dinner date, I did not eat, but she had no such restriction. In person, the imbalanced conversation seemed to interest her only when it concerned her job. Good for her that she loved her work. I love my work too. However, her intense devotion to her work dominated her life such that very little time, energy, or interest seemed to remain for much else, including relationships. I used her love of work as grounds to take her home early so that she could do more work. The date did not appear that fun for either of us. Nevertheless, it was kind of our mutual friend to think that it could, even if it did not lead to a happy ending.

Social Organizations in the Indian Community

Generally speaking, these organizations fall into two categories: family and individual. One type of Indian organization is family-oriented and based on a common feature. For example, the Tamil Sangam is for Tamil families, and the Marati Mandal is for Marati families. All ages and generations are welcome. Other Indian organizations may be organized around a particular interest such as music (e.g., Sruthi and Aradhana). Of course, scanning and scamming the crowd for a mate would be possible at such social events. However, only the truly predatory or relentless would proceed undeterred in such settings.

The second type of Indian social organizations is oriented to the younger generation. One common example is the Indian Student Association (ISA) at many undergraduate colleges and universities in the U.S. These associations vary in size, partly reflecting the numbers of Indian students there. Each ISA also has a different composition of U.S.-raised and native Indians. Particularly the latter group may find the ISA a useful place to meet others with a similar background. U.S.-raised Indians are more likely to have a wider network of friends and family.

Beyond the collegiate scene, another Indian social organization is the Network of Indian Professionals (NetIP). As mentioned on their Website, NetIP began in Chicago in 1990 as a nonprofit organization for South Asians. NetIP is interested in professional, philanthropic, and cultural events plus development.

NetIP has more than 6000 members now and is cyber-connected. For more details, the Website www.netip.org provides an overview of the organization as well as links to the 21 American and two Canadian chapters. Each chapter has a range of activities such as specific programs or trips. Larger social events are open to everyone. The largest gathering is the annual meeting of NetIP in which members of individual chapters and others descend on one central location.

NetIP also provides a shared sense of community. The personality of each chapter may differ. Some are more social and friendly. Others may be less open, especially if the group contains a number of people who have already known each other for a long time. The average age of the group and proportions of married and single people also vary, depending on the chapter.

Each NetIP chapter is certainly interested in enrolling new members. If you are interested, contact the office bearers listed on the Website. To make entering the organization more comfortable, the chapter may have an open house to provide an overview of the organization and give new members a chance to meet.

The key to enjoying any large organization such as NetIP is steady attendance. This will enable you to sift through the mass to find some compatible individuals. Any large organization will have a range of people, and not everyone's interests will align.

Taking on the whole group is potentially more intimidating than a smaller one on a specific activity or trip. A dozen on a ski trip would be more welcoming than a mob of a few hundred in a ballroom. Working on committees allows the larger group to appear more familiar as well.

Professional Organizations

The NetIP is a social group and professional organization. An event at NetIP has people in the same room whose hair, eyes, coloring, and names are in the same league. A shared sense of community is present in other Indian professional organizations. It is partly a question of keeping an eye out for them.

Among physicians, a large group is the American Association of Physicians of Indian Origin (AAPIO), also based in Chicago. One-hundred member associations are throughout the country, and the total membership exceeds 35,000. My own profession has the Indo-American Psychiatric Association (IAPA). The Indo-American Bar Association (IABA) also exists and, not surprisingly, has an active presence in Washington, DC. All such organizations allow a sense of connection to a larger community. It is possible to try out a few organizations and meet new people, not necessarily a new spouse.

At such organizations, it would be too forward to be on an exclusive prowl to find a mate. To wit, some overly eager members of such groups may introduce themselves to strangers at a large function and immediately request personal information such as caste, subcaste, and historical roots in India. Even if those features are important, there are more tactful ways to proceed. Many people would be turned off by these overly forward questions.

Indian Mixers, Nightclubs, and Safety

In areas containing a high concentration of Indians, some large parties are targeted at 20-some year-old Indians. These warehouse-style parties feature dance music that blends Indian and Western influences. The advertisements and the word of mouth circulate, certainly helped by the Internet's popularity and power. The party could be fun, but the reality can be otherwise.

Consider that Indian students are generally studious, and their backgrounds do not lack parental controls. These Indian mixers involve liberation and emancipation.

The desire for a greater experience can entail pursuing liberating and emancipating agents—namely, liquor and other substances. No parents, aunties, or uncles are around this night. In sum, hedonism can reign supreme.

The fall-out of the hedonism can be far from amusing or trivial. A few precautions are appropriate at these mixers, just like any college party. First, watch your intake of alcohol. Obviously, alcohol can impair your judgment. A hangover is benign compared to other outcomes, as discussed below.

A related caution applies to street drugs. Under no circumstances should you put a drink down in a public place and walk away. Always keep it with you or leave it with a previously known and trusted friend. Secondly, it would be foolish to think that you are "safe" among your own "people" and immune to some unpleasantries. Theft can certainly occur. Friends of mine have had purses and expensive leather jackets stolen at such mixers. Presumably, the thieves were our own "people," not trespassers.

To be direct, these mixers can be "meat markets." Those looking to a meet Mr. or Ms. (Indian) Wonderful at such a mixer can certainly face disappointment. Going to a warehouse party does *not* often lead to meeting Mr. or Ms. Right. More likely, it is Mr. or Ms. (Indian) Right Now. In the bright light of morning, the ecstasy has worn off, and this spectacular person may seem quite ordinary indeed. These Indian mixers are no different.

There is nothing wrong with having a big night out with some friends, provided that safety is maintained. A promiscuous meat market is another story. Compromising safety should never be acceptable. Be leery of untoward advances. If a person is not taking no for an answer, be direct with your statements. If that does not work, seek intervention from friends or bouncers. If that is not successful, consider leaving early. Make sure that you are not followed as you leave the party. If you are followed, go to a public area and call the police immediately. Do *not* go to a remote and poorly lit area such as a parking lot.

If a sexual fling is a goal or possibility, be prepared with barrier contraception. Convenient machines dispensing condoms are not always present in the men's and ladies' rooms. There is a difference between using such contraception to prevent pregnancy and preventing sexually transmitted diseases (STDs), including AIDS. In all cases, you got more than you bargained for.

Contraception lowers the risk, but it does not eliminate the chances of pregnancy, STDs, or AIDS. Indians are certainly not immune from pregnancy out of wedlock, STDs, or AIDS. I know of one mixer that resulted in two pregnancies. Yes, two! Did the mixer "cause" the pregnancy? Absolutely not. The two people having unprotected intercourse caused the pregnancy. Did the mixer contribute to a suspension of judgment that made unprotected intercourse more likely? Possibly. It would be totally wrong to assume that all Indian boys and girls are "nice" and not prone to such embarrassing problems that afflict only non-Indians. That erroneous assumption could cost you your health or life.

Violence is another serious concern. The mixer has descendants from the land of Gandhi, but they do not always practice nonviolent strategies to resolve their differences. With enough alcohol and pettiness, violence can certainly break out. At these mixers, plenty of alcohol and pettiness abound. Alcohol can intensify these qualities, making violence even more grotesque. Some Indian mixers have degenerated into gang warfare, accomplishing nothing except a mob of combatants visiting the emergency room.

Indian Bars

Bars oriented to an Indian clientele can be found in cities such as New York that have a sizeable Indian population. At first glance, these bars resemble plenty of other bars: dimly lit, potentially murky, and a number of bottles containing a variety of intoxicating spirits. At closer look, the differences become more apparent. The crowd is predominantly Indian, and the music can be Hindi, bhangra, or fusion. Here also, you are among your "people" in the broadest sense of the term. Unlike mixers, such bars are in fixed locations and open during standard hours. For this reason, the atmosphere may not be as libidinal. Bars have a smaller crowd such that the probability of a wilder time is probably lower. The would-be kinship does not necessarily translate into a having a better time. Meeting a guy or a gal at an Indian bar is comparable to meeting a guy or a gal at a non-Indian bar. Thus, the same cautions are appropriate.

Once, I actually went to one such bar with a group. I found the experience a bit novel. Both inside and outside, it looked like urban America. However, the differences mentioned above were clear. A regular American bar usually does not have three women named "Priya" in attendance.

The volume of the music and atmosphere were not exactly conducive to conversation within our group. Being in a group may have prevented some small talk with others there, but it really did not look like much small talk was occurring generally. Plenty of people were present, but not necessarily enjoying themselves.

Chapter 8

The Internet: Prose, Cons and Warnings

The Internet has become a powerful and relatively recent medium having an influential impact on the Indian community specifically. In India, a strong work ethic and the legacy of the English language have allowed information technology to flourish. Major Indian cities like Bangalore have been transformed in the process. As computers have benefited India, the field in the U.S. has also been enhanced by the Indian community. Large American computer companies such as Microsoft and IBM contain a visible presence of Indians. The latest U.S. census indicates that Silicon Valley in California alone has more than 300,000 people of Indian origin. Obviously, an even greater number of Indians use computers and the Internet.

The Internet has enabled a community of like-minded people. Anyone with a particular interest can find on the Internet plenty of other people with a similar interest. For example, P. G. Wodehouse is a hilarious and incomparable British writer who later settled in New York. Although the fans of Jeeves and others did not seem that numerous to me initially, an Internet search generated an amazing number of Websites devoted to Wodehouse. Full Websites of his quotes and characters span not only English-speaking countries, but others also (e.g., Sweden, Italy, Belgium, and Russia). The Internet cannot turn someone with zero interest in Wodehouse into a devoted fan, but it can link one fan with another. A kinship in cyberspace is possible.

A gathering of like-minded people on the Internet has occurred among the Indian community. Listserves provide news from India or the Indian community abroad. Other listserves offer jokes and puns (e.g., Q: "What is the name of Nitu Singh and Rishi Kapur's child?" A: "Singapore."). A number of Websites offer Indian recipes and even a question and answer section (e.g., "The tone of my *dosai* isn't sufficiently golden. Any suggestions?"). More regional Websites are in an Indian language and English.

Chat Rooms

The Internet can also connect the unattached. Chat rooms are arenas for all people in cyberspace to exchange commentary in live-time, 24 hours a day. Obviously, these people can be anywhere in the world geographically, even if they are linked in cyberspace at the moment. The topic of a chat room can be totally open, or it can involve a particular interest such as politics or sports.

Some chat rooms specifically oriented to single people could be platonic or have an ulterior motive of hooking up. Of course, the "single" person in the chat room may not be truly single. This assumes a certain measure of honesty in self-reporting. Exiting the chat room for a "private" room or exchanging individual e-mail addresses allows more privacy. And the course could continue toward whatever good, bad, or indifferent conclusion.

Indian Chat Rooms

Given the Internet's general scope and the Indian comfort with computers, some chat rooms and Websites devoted to single Indians are especially popular with the young, single crowd. Here, one common feature is being presumably Indian, and the topics for discussion are open.

There is no harm in checking out such a chat room. My own inexperience with them should not deter any curious soul from jumping in. Once, I read a for-warded e-mail that had a transcript of an Indian chat room. The discussants' sense of conflict, humorlessness, and fragility of self overwhelmed me. I have no idea if that type of transcript is uncommon or representative.

General Websites for Singles

Unlike live-time chat rooms, some Websites for singles feature personal adver-tisements and listings that serve to link up two people. Some such Websites are free of charge, while others require fees. The target audience can be all single peo-ple in cyberspace or a specific audience (e.g., residents of Denver or a specific reli-gion).

Single people compose an ad for themselves and submit this and possibly a photo to the Website. Common features include demographic information, a brief self-description, and desirable qualities in a mate (e.g., "30-year-old urban lobbyist and general predator on the prowl. Short, pale, and ugly. Seeking tall, drop-dead gorgeous vixen who does not care about romance, honesty, gun con-trol, election reform, term limits, or the environment. Prenuptial a must. Have your attorney call mine.") Anyone can respond to a tempting listing on the Website. One can also compose an ad for others to respond.

Indian Matrimonial Websites

Some Websites specifically cater to single Indians. Again, the intent and word-ing shifts from "singles Websites" to "matrimonial Websites." These Indian mat-rimonial Websites may resemble those for other singles described above. Other Indian matrimonial Websites can be viewed as a current compliment to such advertisements in printed Indian periodicals such as *India Abroad*.

A master list of Indian matrimonial Websites is provided in Appendix 2. This list was generated by entering "Indian matrimonials" as the key search words in www.google.com. In addition to the master list, the appendix also lists Websites dedicated to some specific Indian communities (e.g., Malayali). Surveying the Websites demonstrated a notable interchange of Indians in the U.S. and those in India. Consequently, the master list does not clearly distinguish residents of the two regions.

Indian matrimonial Websites vary in the level of detail. All cover the basic fields such as age, religion, and area of residence. More comprehensive Websites may have more personal details such as complexion, body type, and salary. An open response here can be revealing and entertaining (e.g., "salary" = "none of your business"). Dropdown menus have fixed choices. A few blank responses may not appear as obvious on a less detailed Website.

On some sites, an internal mechanism allows easy tracking of whom you have approached or rejected. Some Websites have automatic notification if someone meeting your requirements has recently joined. Some even have a "hit" meter to determine how many people checked you out. A low number of hits could lead to self-questioning (e.g., "I'm the cat's meow, but why do I have such few hits?"). Alternatively, a high number of hits could lead to arrogance (e.g., "Of course, others recognize my greatness for what it is."). It is probably best not to check that meter too often.

There is no harm in checking out a chat room or an Indian matrimonial Website. Surveying a few Websites provides a fuller sense of what they are like and the individual listings. One Website's format or a particular listing may be attractive. You can take the plunge and enroll accordingly. Often, it does not even cost anything.

Serial or Simultaneous Approaches

It would be wonderful if stumbling onto one listing leads to an immediate recognition of a long-lost soul mate. However, this discovery is unlikely. More likely, a few listings seem somewhat interesting without an overwhelming sense of "Wow!" Reading along at first pass, keep a list of these initially interesting list-ings.

Then, there are two ways of responding. The slower route is serial: responding to only one person at a time. After hearing a definite "no" or a lack of response, one can proceed to another listing and repeat the process. A more efficient route is simultaneous: responding to several people at the same time and seeing what happens. An even broader simultaneous route is to consider several people on several Websites. If it goes well, one particular contender or a few will be sorted out.

Whether responding to a listing or submitting one, simultaneous enrollment in more than one Indian matrimonial Website maximizes your chances of something "clicking." Being in two places at the same time addresses the reality that a perfect match may not be only on your chosen matrimonial Website. Of course, simultaneous enrollment requires greater time and effort. Keeping careful track of who is who avoids embarrassment. Confusing one person for another would be offensive, understandably. For example, Website #1 with varan #4 has the classicist. Meanwhile, Website #3 with varan #6 has the green-haired surfer.

One byproduct of simultaneous enrollment is the possibility of appearing like a "player." Providing an identical "recycled" response or a duplicated listing will increase the chance of such perceptions.

In sum, the serial and simultaneous approaches offer advantages and disadvantages. Preference for one approach over another may partly depend on personality type, level of organization, and individual comfort. More-cautious or less-organized people may like the ease of tracking only one Website at a time. Bolder or more-organized people may feel more comfortable with simultaneous enrollment.

Responding to someone's listing places the ball in his or her court. By submitting your own listing, the ball is in your court, allowing greater initial control. Responding to a listing *and* posting one for yourself maximizes your chances.

Do's and Don'ts in Responding to a Listing

A few pointers emerge from my own brain and from reading advice and tales on the Internet about these Websites, as outlined in the Bibliography.

(1) *Be nice and polite.* Good manners always help to create a good first impression. This style should be similar to meeting someone in person. For that matter, good manners are always good.

(2) *Amplify.* When you respond to a listing, your user name automatically appears, whether you like it or not. With your user name, the recipient can read your basic demographics and any other information you have provided on the Website. There is no need to repeat it. Provide some information about yourself that you have *not* listed.

(3) *Balance.* Try to be neither too open nor too distant. After all, the recipient is neither an old buddy nor a telemarketer respectively.

(4) *Comment on particulars.* What caught your eye in that person's listing? Stating this directly demonstrates that you are paying attention to features in common (e.g., "In your listing, you mentioned that you enjoy traveling. Where have you been recently? My family and I just returned from a gorgeous vacation in the Caribbean."). This is different than firing off some uninteresting or generic response (e.g., "I saw your ad and you seem like fun.").

(5) *Escape clause.* Although you are clearly a gem, the recipient of your response may not agree or know this yet. In the interests of decency, it is best to offer an exit (e.g., "If you are not interested in proceeding, please let me know."). Obviously, it is important to be true to this promise and not harass that person further. Keep track of those who said "no."

(6) *Anonymity.* Again, the recipient of your response may not be interested in proceeding. Signing off initially with only your user name is anonymous and face-saving. If you must, give only your first name.

Do's and Don'ts in Submitting a Listing of Yourself

Remember that your listing is the reader's first impression of you. You want it to be positive. As given above, some of the "Do's and Don'ts" of responding to a listing apply to the process of submitting one. For example, you should be nice and polite in both instances. Submitting a listing requires some creativity, but not necessarily starting from scratch. Here are some thoughts and recommendations:

(1) *Know your competition.* Read other listings in your own gender. This is your direct and indirect competition. Form a sense of what they are saying and how they are saying it. Also, determine what looks good on a listing and what does not. Using ALL CAPS or a series of!!!!! is annoying.

(2) *Be original.* Surveying your competition will demonstrate some repeated themes (e.g., "nice" or "likes to have fun"). Your listing should have something unique and catchy. A sense of humor helps, even if all do not fully appreciate this. Put your best foot forward, but wear a different type of shoe than everyone else.

(3) *Reflect leisurely.* Give some thought to what exactly you would like to convey about yourself. Write down a first round of ideas when you are in a good frame of mind. Write in a thoughtful and conversational style, not a boring listing of your biography (e.g., "My second grade teacher was Ms.

Tyndall."). Take some time to consider this. Sitting in a lotus posture for deep inspiration may help, but this is not required. Mull over this while doing dishes or sitting in traffic.

(4) *Be honest.* Speak well of yourself, but do not overdo it. Just as you would not appreciate false advertising, do not be a false advertiser. Do not make false claims. If you visit the gym annually, do not pretend to be a daily power-lifter. Omit concerns about being too short, but do not claim to be a giant.

(5) *Emphasize the positive.* Even if misery loves company, no one wants to hear right away that a potential mate's chief interests are terrorizing school kids and throwing rocks at animals in the zoo. Actually, all that would attract a very peculiar attention. Without bending the truth too much, tending to be a killjoy could be recast as "mellow and laid-back," and "hysterical" could be "lively."

(6) *Be conscientious.* By design, your listing requires a computer. On a word processor, translate your preliminary ideas into sentences. Run the spell check to monitor proper usage, such as grammar, capitalization, and punctuation. Your polished final product on the word processor can form your listing on a matrimonial Website. Careless submissions may be ignored or attract people willing to compromise standards. Consider if all of that is okay with you.

(7) *Be concise.* Make sure that the details of your listing is within any word limit on the matrimonial Website. Even if there is no limit, avoid the temptation to ramble. You could appear like a bore at the outset.

(8) *Consult a friend.* Ask a trustworthy friend to read your completed narrative. Preferably, this friend should know you well and offer some constructive comments.

(9) *Set aside at least 24 hours.* After you completed the above steps, put aside your narrative for a day or two at least. Returning to it will give a fresh perspective for editing.

(10) *Consider submitting a photo.* Many Websites indicate that listings with photographs attract more responses than those without them. However, not everyone is comfortable submitting a photo of him or herself. If you do submit one, make sure that you are the subject. It should also be recent and flattering. See also the next chapter for comments on photographs.

(11) *Look at your listing once posted.* Not simply for vanity, see how your listing appears on the Website. Did a misspelled word escape your attention? Does

your photo make you look microscopic or like a fugitive from justice? Does your narrative appear different on the Website than what you intended?

(12) *Revise your profile as you deem fit.* Usually, you can change any dissatisfying aspects of your listing. If necessary, you can also change any information that is no longer accurate.

Internet and Sense of Responsibility

As mentioned above, the Internet neither creates nor destroys. However, it can be a vehicle for creation or destruction. On the positive side, "cyberdating" has successfully paired up some couples. I know one "cyber" couple who eventually married and remain outrageously crazy about each other. The Internet allowed them to come together in the first place. It did not choose the appetizer on the first date. The Internet did not pay for their wedding or their rent. It is not responsible for any of their arguments. Only the two members of the couple can take the credit and blame.

Criminal activities, unusual sexual interests, and divorce existed well before the Internet. Now, the Internet has merely provided easy means of accelerating those existing tendencies and interests. It did not create something from nothing. Websites regarding bestiality will not attract the uninterested. We can choose and not choose to spend time on such Websites.

A bitter man may blame the Internet for the decline of his marriage. However, the blame more squarely goes to the failing relationship itself and the estranged wife who struck up an extramarital affair via the Internet. Again, this person chose to have an affair—not the Internet.

General Caution about Cyberdating

Everyone has heard tall stories about dishonesty on the Internet. The promising new company turns out to be a house of cards. Hot stock tips supposedly coming from a respectable financial organizations turn out to be lies from a bored and sociopathic teenager. We have heard similarly disturbing tales about false self-representation: a self-proclaimed, voluptuous and sexy blonde woman from Beverly Hills is actually a Midwestern, middle-aged male farmer who enjoys cross-dressing. Maintaining a healthy skepticism about honesty and appearances on the Internet can prevent matters from getting out of hand.

Another powerful force in all cyberdating is fantasy. At best, one person knows another persona in cyberspace and possibly a photo. Between contacts, a lot of daydreaming and idealizing can occur. Good appears great, and the resulting perception may distort reality. Cyberspace does not readily demonstrate some faults (e.g., abusing wait staff at restaurants). However, one face-to-face meeting can help determine this.

Released in 2002, the movie *Mitr: My Friend* demonstrates the powerful role of the chat rooms, identity and idealization. An unemanicipated Indian woman derives some comfort by confiding to a stranger in a chat room. An informal cyber relationship develops, as she starts to idealize him. The stranger's identity is increased by fantasy.

Specific Cautions about Cyberdating

Here are some do's and don'ts about cyberdating:

(1) *Slow down!* Test the waters before jumping in head first. One listing may impress you greatly. Indeed, that person may be impressive, but let matters take their course. Submit a friendly reply, but do not overdo it. Sign off using your *user* name. Again, if you must, use only your first name. Generally, keep your wits about you. Carefully consider "going private" off a chat room.

(2) *Create a separate e-mail address.* Consider setting up a totally separate e-mail account for the purposes of cyberdating. For the purposes of this discussion, this will be termed an "auxiliary e-mail account."
Many free e-mail services are available. For your auxiliary account, create a user name that lacks personal information (e.g., gnb@server.com) or a bit quirky (e.g., igroovy@server.com). Your auxiliary e-mail address should not directly reflect your name (e.g., rajkumar@server.com). Use only your last initial, or ask the e-mail server if your last name can be omitted. From this account, send a trial e-mail to a friend to determine how your name appears. Do *not* use a sexually suggestive user name (e.g., libido@emailserver.com). Being libidinal need not be advertised immediately. It is a potentially dangerous set-up. Suggestive user names in chat rooms will also attract that kind of attention.

(3) *Use the Website itself, if possible.* Most matrimonial Websites are structured to send and receive responses within the Website itself. If so, definitely use the Website itself for initial inquiries and exchanges with someone. If the matrimonial Website lacks this function, then use only your auxiliary e-mail address for initial exchanges. If everything is progressing well, then you can switch over to your auxiliary e-mail address, *not* your personal or professional e-mail address.

(4) *Do not give out your telephone number immediately.* Do *not* provide any of your telephone numbers directly on your listing. Initial exchanges with any-

one should be via e-mail only. The exchanges may progress and allow you to feel comfortable considering a telephone conversation. Then, you can choose which number you would like to provide.

Some people may feel comfortable providing only a cellular telephone number. By design, a cell phone is not linked to a precise geographical location. Additionally, it can be turned on or off, as desired. Others may feel comfortable providing a home or office number.

(5) *Possible preliminary steps before calling.* You can use "reverse directory assistance." An operator can then determine if the provided number matches the name of your cyber-friend. Some Websites offer similar services. Before calling, you should block your own number so that it does not appear on caller ID. Alternatively, call from your cell phone.

(6) *Avoid calling toll-free numbers.* Calling any toll-free number will result in your telephone number automatically appearing on that person's bill. Currently, toll-free numbers have the following area codes: 800, 888, 877, and 866.

(7) *Determining age.* As you exchange e-mail, gather a sense of this person's age. Does it match or appear older or younger? Using slang rather than standard English may indicate a younger age. Unfamiliarity with current pop culture may indicate an older person.

Obviously applicable to U.S. citizens only, ask how this person voted in a particular presidential election. The answer will provide some useful information in addition to age. First, it would demonstrate if the person is sufficiently civic-minded to vote in the first place. Second, people typically remember how they voted each time and even where they voted. Third, a vote indicates a political leaning.

(8) *Trust your instincts.* Nietzsche once said that upon meeting someone for the first time, we know everything about that person. At subsequent meetings, we blind ourselves to our own initial wisdom. Although bold, there is some truth in that.

If you have an uneasy sense, pay attention to it. Is this person evasive? Too good to be true? Is this person too boastful to be real? Does the story or history change greatly from one conversation to the next? If you wish, talk to a friend about what is making you uneasy and determine if it is legitimate. General discomfort with a particular person should cancel the proceedings.

(9) *Red flags.* Watch out for the following:

- Refuses to provide home number, despite a long interval of cyber-familiarity.

- Quick discontinuation of phone call (e.g., "I have to go now." Click.). Has the spouse reappeared?

- Abrupt changes in temper or topic (e.g., "So, I am dying to see you…. Uh, no, I can pick up my dry cleaning only on Thursday."). Again, has the spouse reappeared?

- Without notice, long absences from various forms of contact.

- Background noise does not match description. Why does a single person with no kids have a baby crying in the background routinely? Why does it always sound like a party going on? Is any explanation provided?

- Anger if you call randomly.

- Guarded about disclosing personal information, but wants to hear tremendous detail from you.

Structure, No Structure, and Investigative Services

With the traditional or modified Indian approach, the parents play a screening role and provide some security. Totally unacceptable behavior on a date can be reported easily. In fact, it would be surprising if it were *not* reported. For example, if the guy tried to steal the gal's wallet, she can report the attempted theft to her parents. She could also inform his parents directly or her parents could do the same. Even if a mutual friend helped to arrange the date, a similar safety net exists.

"Cyberdating" lacks this screening, security, and the sense of consequences. The best and worst feature of a couple forging its own relationship is that no one else knows. The would-be couple can enjoy increased privacy and not field blunt questions (e.g., "When are you getting married?"). However, there is no internal or external mechanism for redress. If parents heard about attempted theft on a date, they must hear first how exactly the secret date occurred in the first place. Because this disclosure has greater stakes, silence may be an attractive alternative. Thus, any misbehavior may not be punished.

The absence of this safety and structure has prompted the increased number of cautions and warnings about cyberdating given above. Each person can decide what level of caution and comfort fits best individually. If a cyber-exchange is going well, both people may have gathered enough general evidence to indicate that the other seems legitimate and not dangerous.

A more cautious strategy is to enlist outside help. Before proceeding too far, a private investigator can do a background check on the cyber-correspondent. These services are advertised in the yellow pages as well as the Internet. One such service is www.checkmate.com. Each person must decide if the fees are worth it.

In considering a background check in the first place, the bigger question is motivation and intent. Obtaining a background check may be worthwhile to avoid a terrible outcome. However, cyberdating as a process may not suit the cautious or naive. A background check may settle some shady features about the cyber correspondent. It is easier to stop the proceedings with someone who is not this trustworthy. Without trust, nothing in a relationship is possible.

Chapter 9

Making Contact at the Parental Level: Telephone Calls and Dossiers

Contrasting the Western approach, the Indian matrimonial process has more people involved than the couple only. After the crucial determination that both eligible singles wish to proceed, the next question is how the two get in touch. If everyone is local, the process tends to be easy and informal. It is a snap to make a local phone call and meet up without many preliminaries.

My friend Kamal, his parents, a varani, and her parents were in neighboring regions of the same state. They skipped initial formalities and decided to meet up directly. On that day, Kamal met his future wife. All of this was increased by the geographical closeness of all the parties.

In Kamal's "daisy chain," all parties were local. This situation contrasts the one outlined in Figure 7. Each party residing in a different state makes it more difficult. This is not a question of a few local phone calls and driving 20 minutes to meet up.

Figure 7. Daisy Chain across Multiple Sites

Boy's Parents	⟺	Family Friend	⟺	Girl's Parents
(California)		(Illinois)		(Michigan)
⇓				⇓
Boy				Girl
(Texas)				(New Jersey)

Crucial Requirements and Preliminary Contacts with Anyone Anywhere

At the outset, it is essential to determine that the two single people agree to the general Indian matrimonial process *and* with the particular referral in question.

As two crucial requirements to proceed, the answers to both issues must be "yes," as demonstrated in the upper left cell of Table 3.

Table 3. Contingencies and Crucial Requirements

Particular Referral

		Yes	No
Indian Matrimonial	**Yes**	Yes/Yes	Yes/No
Process	**No**	No/Yes	No/No

There are three other possibilities. In the upper right cell, someone may be interested in the Indian matrimonial process, but not with the particular referral. If so, this requires some more "fishing" for more referrals. In the lower left cell, there is no formal interest in the matrimonial process per se, but a chance meeting of an Indian through whatever means leads to a happy outcome.

In the lower right cell, there is no interest with the Indian matrimonial process or a particular referral. In this situation, it is totally meaningless to discuss how to establish contact with a particular referral. Neither the process nor the particular referral is desired. This cell is the exact opposite of the first cell containing the two crucial requirements: agreeing to the Indian matrimonial process and the particular referral.

The Telephone

Indian parents are usually accustomed to the cultural expectation of arranging their son or daughter's marriage. Accordingly, it seems less awkward for a parent to call his or her counterpart with this intent.

When one parent calls a potential sambandhi, it is handy to keep available any information known already. This helps to keep matters straight and can serve as a launch pad for discussion (e.g., "Our friend Charu tells me that your son studied chemistry."). For later retrieval and organization, my father casually took notes on a form containing basic information. Merely as an illustration, this form is included in Appendix 1. It contains information relevant to my parents and me during my search. All the information may not be relevant or valid for everyone, obviously.

Even if my father took notes concurrently, his style during the phone call was conversational. He valued this in others as well. One curious feature of Tamilians is that they do not automatically speak Tamil to one another. Even when one person is talking in Tamil, the response can be in English. Although my father's command of English is definitely above average, he valued the conversation switching to Tamil. One potential sambandhi amused my father by immediately greeting him in Tamil with, "*Solongo, Swami!*" ("Speak, Swami!").

During their chat, my father clarified that the varani in question is actually available. This clarification may seem absurd, but not all seemingly available varanis were truly available. Some were in transition with work or school. A varani stationed in Borneo with the Peace Corps is typically more concerned about matters other than being single. In other cases, the presence of a current varan or competition was stated plainly or implied. Even if the varani had no such overt encumbrances, her parents may have wanted to check with her before proceeding. And that is fine.

By the end of his chat, my father also discussed the possibility of exchanging dossiers, as described below more fully. Even if he covered a lot of information on the phone already, he found the dossier a useful supplement to the conversation. Being a man of science, my father would clarify when exactly the potential sambandhi planned to send the dossier. Organized folks were prepared to send it immediately. My father asked the less organized and more vague when exactly they would be ready so that my father could send my dossier around the same time. He appreciated organization, punctuality, and honesty in potential sambandhigal.

Lastly, my father had a log sheet to enter the date of the telephone call and the gist of what they discussed (e.g., 1/6/99. Spoke to Herman Munster, friend of the Addams. Telephone number (123) 456-7890. Will call back re: Marilyn within 1 week. Address: 1313 Mockingbird Lane, Camelot, NJ 09999). Supplementing the earlier form, his log sheet on Microsoft Excel was useful in keeping and retrieving some details.

Standard Mail and e-mail

A course and approach similar to the above apply to printed matrimonial ads in periodicals such as *India Abroad*. First, the two crucial requirements must be satisfied, and the parents usually initiate the contact with a letter, telephone call, or e-mail.

Responding by standard mail or e-mail is more deliberate, requiring greater thought than a less-formal "real-time" conversation on the telephone. For this reason, more thought and preparation go into composing a response, as elaborated below.

Dossiers

Although this term has general use, here *dossier* refers to a collection of documents used in the Indian matrimonial process. It may contain only a cover letter. Possible additional items include a separate sheet of biodata, horoscope, and a photograph. Each item will be discussed in turn.

Cover letter

As implied, this letter provides an overview. Typically, this letter is composed in English. At least this is true with the Tamil community. The letter often begins by stipulating how this contact came to be (e.g., "I saw your advertisement in *Talkative Tamilian Telegraph.*"). Alternatively, the cover letter can follow up an introductory chat (e.g., "It was nice talking to you on Wednesday about a potential alliance between our children Sita and Ram.").

This cover letter usually lists the family's origins in India. In a related way, caste and subcaste may be given. There may be details on how and where the family has settled. The parents' occupations and some basics about the siblings may be given as well.

After all this background, there is information specifically related to the varan or varani. Basics include when and where the person was born and raised. Educational history and profession are also noted. Lastly, there is a discussion of the person's personality, leisurely pursuits, interests, and qualities desired in a mate.

Pointers on Cover Letters

The general content of a cover letter has been described above. Implied in this discussion are some do's and don'ts. Your cover letter says something about yourself, and you would like to create a positive impression. Being conscientious and adding a personal touch improve those chances.

Here are some specific recommendations:

(1) *Take your time.* Just like the recommendations given on submitting a listing of yourself on a matrimonial Website, take some time to consider the contents of the letter. What would you like to convey, and how are you conveying this?

(2) *Handwritten versus Alternates.* The personal touch provided by elegant penmanship can create a particularly good impression. It always impressed my father. If you are going to write a letter by hand, your handwriting should be legible at a minimum. If your handwriting is shocking or illegible—you know who you are—use another means to write a letter. In this age of computers, you have no excuse.

(3) *Word processors.* As discussed earlier, using a word processor has a number of advantages. The computer program can run a spell check and grammar check. Take advantage of those simple and quick features. Revising text is also easy. Questions about proper English usage can be referred to a knowledgeable friend. Appropriate changes to your document can be done painlessly.

A word-processed document can provide a template of fixed details such as history and education. To send the letter to a particular person, most of the work is already finished. Then only minimal work is necessary in writing a name, address, an introductory paragraph, and some appropriate details.

(4) *Stay with only one format.* The letter should be entirely handwritten or entirely printed by a computer. If you are using a computer, a handwritten insert on the printout looks messy. Once again, take the extra minute to make that correction on a computer document itself and generate a polished printout.

(5) *Use good quality paper.* Use a reasonable font for the printout. Use only one font throughout the document. Select a clear and common font such as Times New Roman, Arial, Courier, or Helevetica. A font size of 10- or 12-points provides easy legibility. Smaller fonts can appear shifty or hushed. Larger fonts appear childish. Multiple fonts in the same letter may appear sloppy or bizarre.

(6) *Stationery.* India and many parts of the world produce gorgeous stationery that is suitable for handwritten correspondence. The actual choice of paper is less important than the contents. Unruled stationery is fine, provided that the writing is even and legible.

I am still unsure what to make of a cover letter that had a border of dancing animals. If my family were Muslim or Jewish, the pigs in ballet poses would have been outright offensive.

Do not use paper torn from a spiral notebook. Do not use stationery that contains your professional letterhead. Even if the letterhead is nice or impressive, a matrimonial cover letter is not exclusively a business matter.

(7) *Printing.* Using a laser printer is elegant and appropriate. Dot matrix is outdated. Printing a fresh letter each time looks better. If you lack access, laser printing at photocopy stores costs less than $1 per page.

(8) *Photocopying.* If you wish to use a less personalized route, you could make photocopies of a general letter to be sent to prospects. This could be addressed to no one or a generic "Dear Advertiser." A light highlighter mark on one corner distinguishes the original from a copy, because a lightly highlighted area does not copy in black ink. Whenever necessary, copy the original. In whatever generation, a copy of copy is never as crisp as copying the original.

(9) *Signature.* Signing the letter is more personal than a photocopy of a signature.

Standard Mail versus e-mail

A classified matrimonial advertisement may list an e-mail address for contact rather than a street address. The actual responses are the same. Again, if a standard cover letter is saved on a word processor, one can cut and paste a reply to an e-mail address. Adding some personal points will make this appear less impersonal.

Biodata, Résumé, or CV

As discussed above, the cover letter often covers the demographic information that would qualify as "biodata," the term traditionally used in this context. As an option, some dossiers summarize this information on a separate sheet in outline format. Typically listed features include: date of birth, family origins, parental details, caste, subcaste, education, employment, siblings, and leisure interests.

At times, this outline can be a concise summary attached to the text of the cover letter. At other times, the sheet of biodata seems business-like and resembles a résumé or academic curriculum vitae (CV). Without any attempt at disguise, some dossiers contain the same résumé used in seeking employment.

It is important to remember the dossier's purpose: an introduction to a possible mate. The fine points of your career are irrelevant. Successfully completed exams (e.g., driving license in Brazil) and professional certifications (e.g., board-certified in addiction medicine) do not matter. Those details on a résumé may interest a future employer and land a job. However, do not mix business with pleasure.

An employer usually does not care about your ancestral village (e.g., "If he hails from Maharajapuram as I do, he must be good! Hire him immediately!"). A prospective mate usually does not care about specific professional activities (e.g., "Landing a contract with Steveland Morris Judtland is impressive! I'll marry her immediately!"). Remember the purpose.

Horoscope

Another optional item in a Hindu dossier is what is known in Tamil as *jathagam* (pronounced "JAA-tha-gum). This term is loosely translated as "horoscope." The Indian system is much more intricate and more involved than the Western zodiac. A jathagam's details involve planetary and other celestial positions at the time of birth. This system serves not only as the basis of predicting the individual's future, but also determining a potential couple's astrological compatibility.

In the past, an astrologer determined the compatibility of two horoscopes, required for any engagement and marriage. An astrological incompatibility would halt the proceedings between these two people. All parties accepted this final decision, because literally no earthly means could correct this problem. The search for a mate would begin anew. There would be continued hope of finding a person with a compatible horoscope.

Astrological compatibility also allows the priests to determine an auspicious hour and date for a wedding. Some key events in the ceremonies must be performed during that time, known in Tamil as *muhurtham* (pronounced "MOO-hoor-thum"). Also known as *muhoorth* in Sanskrit, this is defined as "a moment, period of time (auspicious or otherwise), lasting 48 minutes" (Apte 1970).

The current value placed in the compatibility of horoscopes can vary. If valued, the whole process centers on a favorable astrological determination. Like my own, some unions have proceeded without consulting an astrologer. Even without this consultation, the couple must observe the muhurtham at the wedding. Ours did.

To help the observant, some dossiers give a full jathagam or the locations of its key elements. Knowing the place, date, and time of birth can allow any astrologer to generate a jathagam to determine the compatibility of a potential couple. These days, a computer program determines the same.

Including a full jathagam in a dossier is optional. The observant will welcome this useful and necessary information. The unobservant consider it extraneous. The less observant party can provide enough details to allow the more observant party to create a jagatham.

Photographs

Printed matrimonial advertisements commonly include, "Photo a Must." Listings on the Internet can also include the person's own photograph and request the same from respondents. In fact, several matrimonial Websites state that listings with photographs generate more responses than those without them. Even if photographs are requested, not every respondent sends one.

Within the Indian matrimonial process, perhaps no other issue generates more conflict and controversy. In favor of photographs is the argument that they provide a face to the name and humanize the process. As splendid as the text may be, appearance is also a part of a person, no different than a voice or laugh. Photographs also betray the central reality that people must be able to envision themselves with this other person. This reality need not be too vain or an excessive focus on looks. For one reason or another, not everyone can imagine being with everyone else.

Generally, couples marry in a comparable level of attractiveness, as will be discussed in later chapters. Beautiful marries beautiful. Mediocre marries mediocre, and so on. A photograph can help determine if a potential compatibility or attraction could exist.

Of course, one problem with this is an accurate view of one's self. At the risk of being unbearable, some may view themselves as more attractive than the consensus. On the other hand, some may view themselves as less attractive than the consensus and risk excessive humility and a poor self-image.

Arguing against photographs is the loss of privacy. It is one matter to be "Lakshmi" from Houston, a faceless gal in a sea of similarly named individuals in a large city. A photo converts this Lakshmi into a more directly recognizable person. Photographs can also encourage excessive attention to physical attributes, not other personal features. Some people do not photograph well. I do not. Photographs often make me look goofy or as if I have just been rudely cut off in traffic.

As photographic equipment can vary in quality, so can amateur photographers, reflected in the photographs themselves. Pocket-sized cameras with film are very easy to use. They are called "point and shoot" for a reason. More advanced single-lens reflex (SLR) cameras generate better photographs. Technological improvements have allowed operating a newer SLR camera painlessly. The latest development is the digital camera.

Recommendations about Photographs

Those who oppose photographs can proceed with someone who has a similar or no opposition. If the objection to photographs is not strong, those entering "the market" would be well-served to have available several copies of recent photographs of themselves.

Advanced availability of such photographs will allow them to accompany any immediate request for a dossier. Scrounging up something at the last minute can look exactly that way.

At the risk of being redundant and picky, here are some recommendations:

(1) *Studio versus self.* Studio photographs are more formal and polished than those taken by most amateurs. After all, one could stay at home, be photographed as is with a single-use camera, and the process would be less than $10. If you are uncomfortable taking photographs or do not have a good camera, consider studio photographs. Computers in photo studios make this process faster and easier than yesteryear.

(2) *Digital versus film.* A digital image can exist in a variety of forms, including a digital camera, a scanned photograph on CD-ROM, or an attachment to an e-mail. The best and worst feature of any digital medium is its versatility. Sending e-mail with an attached photo is very convenient. However, the

recipient may not keep that to him or herself. It would be easy to forward the photo to friends and family.

TO: the_world@allcyberpace.com

FROM: vavoom@server.com

RE: Hey! Check out this morsel's photo!

It is worth considering an individual's comfort with unauthorized, but potential distribution.

(3) *Lighting.* Photographs in natural light are typically better than those taken with a flash. Evenly diffuse natural light produces consistent results. A bright day is ideal for a photograph. A blazing day with intense sun can cause one to squint and scowl, as demonstrated by multiple photographs of me in India. Smiling does help smooth these facial expressions.

(4) *Background.* In addition to the person being photographed, consider what else will appear in the photograph. A photo at the zoo may accidentally capture an orangutan. Do not make it difficult to distinguish which ape wants to marry. A photo at home may include disorganized materials on a coffee table or a bookshelf in disarray. Set up the background and environment for the photograph and center the subject.

(5) *Clothing and Appearance.* Women often wear Indian clothes in these photographs, while men usually wear Western clothes. Whatever the style, the clothes should be presented well. Even if you are a slob, overcome this tendency at least once for a photo. It is better to err on the side of formality: no excessively revealing clothes, no t-shirts, no blue jeans, and no blatant commercial logos (e.g., dot.com companies or pesticides). Seduction, informality or financial promotions can occur later, if at all.

Hair should be combed in a comfortable and familiar style—nothing "experimental." Men should shave or lack transitional facial hair. Men who have a mustache or beard should have them appropriately groomed or trimmed. The same is true for women. Overall, the photograph should flatter the person.

(6) *Appropriate distance.* The photograph should not be so close that dental cavities and skin pores are visible. On the other hand, they should not be so far that it resembles a puzzle of "Where's Waldo?" Determine a comfortable length that portrays at least the head and shoulders. Half-body or full-length shots are also fine.

(7) *Single versus multiple people.* Matters are simple in photographs portraying only one person—what you see is what you get. Sometimes, a dossier may have a family photograph. If so, the varan or varani should be identified. A

huge arrow or bull's-eye etched with a china marker is artistically unpleasant. An indication in the cover letter or back of the photo is fine (e.g., "Our daughter Bharathi is on the left wearing red.").

(8) *Self-portrayal.* One matrimonial listing on the Internet featured a photo of a gleeful guy waving from his sporty convertible. In a studio shot, another guy wore a red and black leather jacket while leaning earnestly on a motorcycle helmet. Yet another featured a gal with a dreamy look while raising a glass of wine invitingly. In respective order, these photographs may preferentially attract a gold-digger interested in cruising, biker fans of Michael Jackson during his *Thriller* days, and lushes.

Think about what your photograph says about you, and the kind of person you wish to attract.

(9) *Write your name on back.* For clarity, write your name on the back of the photograph. Using a permanent marker such as a "Sharpie" will not ruin the front of the photograph. You can also write your address if you would like the photograph returned.

(10) *Copies.* As discussed already, the search for a mate can be vast and requires a broad net. Thus, it is helpful to have multiple copies of these photographs available, not just one. Copies of studio photographs are easily ordered. If it is a film-based amateur photograph, copies based on the negative are also possible. Alternatively, photocopy stores and other places have computers that scan any single photo to generate a sheet of duplicates. It is easy and not that expensive.

Chapter 10

Behaving Yourself: Responding at the Peer Level, Telephone Calls, and Etiquette

Previous chapters have described three sources of referrals: self, peer, and parental. If there is mutual interest with any referral, the next step is responding. In cyberspace and self-referrals, the source of the referral and forum for response are often identical. Namely, a person placing a listing on a matrimonial Website most likely expects initial responses from that Website. At an Indian mixer, a person who uses a saucy pick-up line to begin conversation does not usually run away after providing a business card with an e-mail address.

First Things First

As mentioned in earlier chapters, two crucial requirements must be satisfied: both eligible singles must agree to the overall Indian matrimonial process and proceeding with this particular referral. The answer to both criteria must be "yes." If even one answer is "no," there is nothing further to discuss. No meaningful relationship begins under such pressure.

The person may agree with the Indian matrimonial process, but needs time to consider a particular referral. There is no harm in gaining this clarification. In fact, the extra time may be worthwhile in that only truly interested parties would be coming together.

Daisy Chain and Transitioning

As illustrated earlier, the "daisy chain" contains an array of people: the matchmaker, parents, boy, and girl. Ultimately, the only "eligible" parties are the boy and girl. As illustrated in Figure 6 earlier, a shift in contact must occur from the ineligible people to the eligible couple. The boy and girl must be chummy and more for the potential sambandhigal to become actual sambandhigal, even if the latter are highly compatible. The children can establish contact in one of three major ways:

(1) *Telephone.* The would-be sambandhigal were often involved in the preliminaries. In exchanging their children's telephone numbers, a quick follow-up conversation between the two would-be sambandigal can be helpful in two ways before boy and girl attempt to talk.

First, "phone tag" between boy and girl may be reduced. Usually, the boy calls the girl first, demonstrating that gentleman-like behavior is not entirely dead. A parental-level conversation can determine a general or specific time that each offspring is available. Designating an "appointment" for a telephone call may be artificial or business-like. However, I believe that this is much better than exchanging rounds of messages on answering machines. Such an "appointment" also prevents a conversation from occurring in the absence of something better to do (e.g., "No one wants to go out tonight, so I'll try to talk to this person.").

Preliminary contact between the two would-be sambandhigal can be helpful in a second way: reducing ignorance and surprise. Assuming both sets of sambandhigal have an open relationship with their children, the varani can be briefed before talking with a particular varan with whom she has agreed to proceed. This way, his call does not alarm her completely. Such a parental-level clearance is helpful, but not a guarantee.

After such a clearance, I once called a varani who was supposed to be eagerly awaiting my call. After I introduced myself, it was quickly obvious that she had no idea who I was. Her reaction indicated that I could have been a close student of Jack the Ripper and skillfully obtained her phone number. I spoke to her only once. She was obviously not prepared or interested in talking to me, and I saw no reason to force the issue.

(2) *Cyber-connection.* Exchanging e-mail addresses can supplement telephone numbers or an independent means of establishing initial contact. A boy or girl can compose e-mail at any time, and there is no equivalent to phone tag with answering machines. The couple could exchange e-mail to establish an "appointment" to talk on the phone or meet directly.

(3) *Direct contact.* Prior to meeting directly, chatting on the telephone or exchanging e-mail is common. Of course, the couple could meet directly without any such contact. This is comparable to receiving a confidential message and secret assignment from high command (e.g., "You will shower, wear presentable clothes, and give the secret sign at Curry Cravers at 7 PM on Saturday. Your exotic date will be wearing a rose and ask if diamonds are a girl's best friend."). It worked in *Mission Impossible* after all.

Telephone Manners, The $64-million question, and Second Phone Calls

The telephone is ultimately a common and important medium of establishing and maintaining contact. If it were not, the social and business worlds would have abandoned it long ago. Some comments about telephone calls have been implied or mentioned in various sections in this chapter and previous ones. To review and continue the discussion, here are some specific recommendations:

(1) *Preparation.* If truly interested, it is helpful for each boy and girl to know a bit about the other before the phone call. A dossier can provide this knowledge. At a minimum, each person should know the other's name and location.

(2) *Perception.* Attitude about the phone call can play an important role. A study by Snyder and colleagues (1977) found that on an initial phone conversation, men were friendlier and more social toward women who attracted them in whatever way. By implication, they were less friendly toward less appealing women. As described in later chapters, attraction is not limited to desirable physical qualities.

(3) *Time to Call.* Everyone is "busy" and "tired" these days. There is never a perfect time to call. If there is enough commitment to the overall process, one will find time and energy. Between 7 PM to 9 PM on weekdays is usually a reasonable time to catch people. The difference between the beginning and end of a phone call is less pronounced for the concise. For the more verbal, starting a call at 9 PM can lead to a delayed bedtime.

Not everyone has the same sleeping habits. The vast majority of Indians are early risers and "sleeping in" is 5:30 AM. Thus, calling at 6 AM must be okay. It is not! Just because someone is probably awake, calling even at 8 AM on Saturday is not necessarily welcome. Let that person enjoy some sleep or the calm of the morning. The only exception is a specific request for a call at an odd time.

(4) *Introduction.* Despite these enlightened times, it is typically up to the boy to call the girl. Even if she is expecting his call, it is helpful for the boy to introduce himself by name and location (e.g., "This is Vasu from Phoenix."). He can add how he received her name and number (e.g., parents, mutual friend, or an advertisement). This information can help her place him. If she cannot, this ignorance may be telling.

(5) *"Is this a good time?"* Even after following all the recommendations above, it is polite to ask directly if this is a good time. One obvious reason is that it

may not in fact be a good time (e.g., pressure cooker just detonated). If it is not a good time, honor that. However, it is helpful to take an extra minute to determine a mutually convenient time for a follow-up call and who will call whom.

Asking if this is a good time also allows a face-saving exit for the uninterested. It is crucial that each is interested in the other. Third parties may provide guarantees to that effect (e.g., "My daughter does nothing but stare at the phone hoping that your son will call."). However, reality may be otherwise. An uninterested person would not welcome a phone call from an unappealing imposer. Terminating an unwelcome phone call early benefits everyone. The caller has not been traumatized or wasted too much time or money. The recipient of the phone call has also saved time and not caused too much offense.

(6) *Awkward.* It clears the air for the boy or girl to state plainly that this phone call is awkward. After all, it *is* artificial. Consider the common preliminaries. One set of parents spoke to another set of parents. Perhaps the call is the culmination of a response to a personal ad on the same page as "motel for sale." Possibly, a dossier was assembled and exchanged. Alternatively, a friend or family member thought that this phone call would be a good idea. No matter how consensual or prepared, it is awkward.

(7) *Chat for the sake of chatting.* Rather than being totally intense, assume a more casual approach to the phone call. Consider it like small talk at an informal party. In fact, knowing some preliminary information about the other person makes this easier than some totally speculative small talk with a complete stranger (e.g., "Who is your favorite Beatle?").

As an example of how *not* to proceed, I once endured a painful questioning with a rigid varani who seemed to apply a business model to her personal life. In fact, I remember that call as a relentless drilling for information rather than an actual conversation (e.g., "So, what are you looking for? What else? What else?"). She stopped just short of asking me what talents and services I would bring to her "company."

(8) *Be nice.* At any stage in the process, it never hurts to be polite. Remember your manners. Do not say "huh?" Say, "Excuse me" or "Pardon." Interrupting is rude and intrusive. Even if you are prone to nastiness, try to overcome your base tendencies. Alternatively, hope that this person is equally nasty, and everything clicks.

(9) *Avoid being obnoxious and too personal.* In the initial phone call, asking overly personal questions is inappropriate (e.g., "How much do you earn?"

or "Have you ever had plastic surgery?"). If an actual relationship develops, talking about more personal matters would not be as bold (e.g., "Would you like to have children?").

In my opinion, the most obnoxious question ever posed in an initial phone call was the boy asking the girl if she is a virgin. True story. They never spoke again.

(10) *Expand on bits of information.* As mentioned above, expanding on basic information is an easy way to generate conversation (e.g., "I understand that you went to school in New England. What was your experience like?" or "What do you like about your current city?"). This recommendation seems obvious, but it is worth keeping in mind.

The broader the question, the greater the chance of discussion. For example, asking, "What do you like to do when you are not working?" is more open-ended than, "What movie did you see last?" Some universal questions can also promote conversation (e.g., "Tell me about your family.").

(11) *The $64-million question*: "How did you declare your candidacy in the Indian matrimonial process?" If the situation presents itself, it is informative to ask how exactly a person agreed to proceed with the Indian matrimonial process. The answer can help determine two major issues. First, is this person actually willing and interested in proceeding? Force and reluctance to proceed may come out in the answer (e.g., "My parents put me up to this."). Second, the answer to this question tells you a bit about this person. Is the answer careless or not well reasoned? Is this person actually astonished to receive a phone call from a total stranger? Alternatively, is the answer balanced and thoughtful, indicating some free will?

In my case, answering the $64-million question required a warning. I would caution the questioner that my answer is at least a ten-minute discourse with examples that included the philosopher Georg Hegel and the writer Ralph Ellison. If the varani were not terrified, I proceeded with the answer. My response revealed some features about myself. I entered the Indian matrimonial process of my own free will. Dead German philosophers and Southern Black writers can strike a chord in my thinking. This preview would duly warn any varani willing to continue contact with me.

Another feature of the $64-million question is timing. As much as I think that this question is entirely reasonable, when to ask this question is another matter. Asking this question on the first phone call is not required. Discuss this whenever the opportunity presents itself naturally. If the opportunity does not occur with the first call, it will recur.

(12) *Determine if a second call is worthwhile.* The first phone call is merely a "hello" or "howdy," if you like. The course of the conversation should determine if there is mutual interest in second conversation. Determine a good time to talk again, and who will call whom. As I tended to make the first call, I usually asked the varani to call me next. Placing the ball in her court was mainly motivated by providing a face-saving exit. If I misread the situation, she did not have to call me back, rather than enduring another unwelcome phone call from me.

I once called a varani and asked her if it was a good time. She said that it was, but she needed to turn off the video. I offered to call after she finished the movie. In declining my offer, she confessed that she was watching a Marx Brothers movie for the "umpteenth" time. Her confession impressed me. My family and I are devoted fans of the Marx Brothers, and our delight has not declined after "umpteen" viewings. Moreover, I appreciated the varani's willingness to take the time to accept my call. That first phone call established a sufficient foundation to proceed to a second phone call.

If the first conversation did not flow well, it may be painful to repeat the exercise. I once spoke to a varani who worked with computers. Her radically different hobby was surfing the Web. Her interests in reading also related to computers.

In spirit, computers for that varani were like shrimp for the character Bubba Blue in the movie, *Forrest Gump* (1994). Forrest's colleague Bubba loved all forms of shrimp: "shrimp kabobs, shrimp Creole, shrimp gumbo, pan fry, deep fry, stir fry, pineapple shrimp, lemon shrimp, coconut shrimp, pepper shrimp, shrimp soup, shrimp stew, shrimp salad, shrimp and potatoes, shrimp burgers, and shrimp sandwich."

A dedicated shrimp man would be happiest with a shrimp woman. I do not eat shrimp. Independent of shrimp, a dedicated computer gal would be happiest with a computer guy. I am not that guy. I like and marvel at computers, but I like doing other things as well. One stilted "conversation" with her was enough.

Although there have been a few references to rejections here, this topic will be discussed at greater length in Chapter 14.

Chapter 11

Establishing Contact: Family Gatherings and Ensemble Meetings

In yesteryear in India, some young couples met for the first time on the wedding day itself. This type of arrangement was more common in Indians presently 55 years of age and older. Even now, the bride at a Bengali wedding enters holding two leaves to cover her eyes while female escorts guide her, clearing any obstacles such as seated people and plants. Close to the groom, she removes the leaves for the couple's "first viewing." Although this "first viewing" no longer matches reality, this feature is retained in weddings as a formality.

More recently, young couples in India have met at least once before the marriage. At the formal initial meeting, the boy and his family typically visited the girl and her family. House gifts customarily included fruits and flowers. When the entourage arrived, the girl was often absent initially and made an entrance later, either alone or escorted. Some general discussion ensued, but a direct exchange between boy and girl was not totally common.

Certainly, there may be some general discussion occurring as if people are absent (e.g., "Where did your son study?" while the boy is sitting right there). This is akin to a judge asking the defense attorney for the defendant's age directly in front of the defendant. In a potentially awkward situation, the boy's family may ask about the girl's talents. For example, my grandparents were concerned that one of their daughter's inability to sing may affect her eligibility to marry. As chance would have it, a suitor and his family did ask her to sing during their visit. Not missing a moment, her more musically gifted sister sang instead. The switch did not prove to be a crisis, because the young couple married soon thereafter. My aunt and uncle have remained married more than sixty years.

More recently in India, the interchange between potential bride and groom became freer and less structured. The traditional, initial meeting may have had a more relaxed atmosphere. Afterward, either boy or girl could decline to proceed, a change in the historical standard of the boy and his family retaining the upper hand. If the boy and girl decided to proceed, the couple may have seen each other again before the wedding.

After their formal introduction and engagement, my parents-in-law actually went on a "date" once. To minimize scandal, one female relative from each side accompanied them. These two women ensured further decency by sitting between the couple in the movie theater.

Backdrop, The Present, and Ensemble Meetings

The Indian generation currently in their sixth decade or greater may have started married life as strangers, but many created solid and loving relationships. Certainly, some marriages have not been successful, but many positive examples exist.

That generation would be comfortable and familiar with the children pursuing any course that resembles its own. These parents have typically viewed arranging their child's marriage as their responsibility. They may want both sets of families to meet initially, not just boy meeting girl individually. For ease in discussion here, a meeting involving the boy's and girl's families will be termed "ensemble meeting."

Sambandhigal Only

Just as the young couple can meet without parental supervision, the potential sambandhigal can meet without their children's presence, even if the children are the reason for the meeting. Each set of parents gathers a sense of the other set, under the assumption that the fruit does not fall far from the tree. Of course, they will discuss their own child's virtues and note potential areas of compatibility.

The Indian sense of geography can be skewed. The presence of relatives or a known contact can determine the itinerary, not their actual physical location and intervening distances. My father-in-law has taken flights from the West Coast to Chicago "via" the Eastern Seaboard to visit some people.

In this spirit, one potential sambandhigal once visited my parents on the grounds that they were "passing through" the area, although their origin and destination were beside the point. When the two sets of parents met, their daughter and I were absent. That uncle greedily consumed my mother's Indian snacks and practically eliminated the supply that she originally considered to be more than enough. She was amazed at how noisily one man could chew. Without clear purpose, this uncle often had a darting and searching gaze around the house. My father did not know if this uncle were appraising my parents' house against his own or if he intended to return under the cover of darkness to loot the joint.

These questions were never answered clearly. A short time after this meeting, my parents received an abrupt letter from him canceling the proceedings.

Ensemble Meetings: Pro and Con

Comfort with the idea of an ensemble meeting can vary. The U.S. generally places a greater emphasis on the individual rather than the family, and the prospect of an ensemble meeting may seem uncomfortable or old fashioned. Meeting a stranger with the clear possibility of marriage is strange enough without the presence of other family members. An ensemble meeting can interject too many opinions. By contrast, meeting one-on-one seems preferable for such people.

Favoring ensemble meetings is the Indian assertion that one does not marry just another person, but one marries into a family. At the outset, the eligible couple can derive a sampling of the other's family as well. My former professor's wife holds that his family is another reason that she married him. She felt that he comes from good stock, and they would accept her. Based on more than 25 years of marriage, she has been correct. On the other hand, my former professor said that he married his wife *despite* her family. Incidentally, none of them is Indian.

The family often hears about the date later anyway, and an ensemble meeting saves one phone call. Seeing how the family interacts can also provide a perspective on the family as a whole. The parents' conduct and character provide some insight to the children. Of course, the couple must feel at ease with each other. Each person can see directly if marrying into this family would be comfortable.

It is also important to not hold the family entirely against a person. People have no choice in determining their parents and siblings. If some family members are not the finest, it is not the varan or varini's fault. The question is how much this impacts the single person. A completely foul sibling is not too disruptive if that person surfaces only at Memorial Day and Thanksgiving. Merely being related does not guarantee identical character. Within any family, there can be great variability. This is certainly true in my family. If we find some relatives questionable, who knows what they think about us? Probably, the feeling is mutual.

Flexibility in Individual versus Family

As implied above, some people may have strong feelings about meeting individually versus an ensemble meeting. Those who insist on an ensemble meeting alienate those who insist meeting individually and vice versa. Strong arguments favoring each approach may cause some leads to end prematurely. Being flexible decreases the chance of such alienation.

An open approach balances the two. Initially, the boy and girl can chat. If it progresses well, the two can discuss whether to meet individually or as an ensemble. This discussion can be informative. For example, one former varani's selective disclosures to her family contrasted my family's general knowledge about what is going on with me. If that varani and I had an ensemble meeting, her father and sisters must first learn what his wife and daughter have been doing behind the scenes. Raising that topic itself would require some courage. Then only could arrangements for the ensemble meeting occur.

East versus West: Character and Timing

In the West, two people meet on their own, date, and become an "item." If a relationship develops, the boy can introduce the girl to his family, and she can do the same with hers. Here, an ensemble meeting often occurs only if the relationship is moving toward an official commitment. A well-planned wedding must involve coordination and contact between the two families. Indeed, I learned this painful lesson after attending some disorganized and oddly competitive weddings.

The classical Indian approach has the exact opposite chain of events. Two families come together. The couple marries and then becomes an "item." Historically, not even marriage resulted in the couple being alone, as the bride went to live with her husband and his family.

With the Indian community in the U.S., it is possible to balance the two approaches. At first, the Indian custom can prevail in which the parents do some groundwork to discover a varan or varani. Once discovered, a more Western custom can be activated, as the boy and girl establish direct contact and possibly meet up. If a relationship develops, introductions to the family are possible.

Even with such a balanced Indian-Western model, there are two continued major differences: character and time frame. Consider a candid relationship with good boundaries between an Indian parent and child. The Indian parent may hear in general terms about the child's dates. Merely by virtue of being Indian, the parent will soon recommend that the child invite the significant other to come over for dinner (e.g., "Why don't you ask her to come over for *puri*?"). The other set of parents may make a similar recommendation (e.g., "I can make *puri* too. Why don't you ask him to come over?"). If this introduction goes well, the Indian parents are usually eager for the young couple to progress and formalize the relationship. As a crude summary, you can take the person out of India, but you cannot take India out of the person.

With a finite goal of marriage, the early question is if this relationship can progress toward such a commitment. Compared to Western standards, all of this seems rushed. By historical Indian standards, all of this seems too leisurely.

Atmospheric Conditions

The nature of an ensemble meeting depends on the situation. In one circumstance, the young couple may have no prior contact and enter the ensemble meeting "cold." Obviously, the sambandhigal have been in contact for that meeting to occur in the first place. This circumstance is the most formal and least familiar. The only links may be phone calls between the sambandhigal and possibly an exchange of dossiers. My wife and I actually first met cold in an ensemble meeting.

A cold ensemble meeting could be partly changed if the young couple talked on the phone prior to meeting. This way, both sambandhigal and the young couple have made an initial acquaintance with presumably enough justification to meet. Accordingly, the atmosphere and conversation at the ensemble meeting could be less formal and warmer.

The atmosphere would be entirely different if an ensemble meeting occurred as a natural progression of the young couple's courtship. This ensemble meeting would entail fewer introductions from one stranger to another. The increased sense of familiarity provides the least formal, and potentially the most relaxed setting.

Where and How

As mentioned above, the historical approach in India with ensemble meetings was clear in that the girl's family hosted the boy's. The situation is not as clear with the Indian community in the U.S. This issue partly depends on geography. An ensemble meeting closest to most people's locations is most practical, regardless of boy's side or girl's side. It may involve some maneuvering and coordinating to determine a time and place to meet to suit everyone.

When my future wife and I first met, we were living about an hour and half away from each other. My parents were about two hours away from my place. Her parents were in another time zone. My parents drove, and her father took a flight to attend an ensemble meeting at my place. It went well and had a positive outcome, obviously. In fact, my father-in-law believes that his attending the ensemble meeting played a positive role in his daughter's eventual marriage.

Meeting at one person's home is most common. This requires more work for the host, but it provides the most privacy. In my opinion, the finest food in the world is not in any restaurant, but comes from the kitchens of good cooks everywhere. Without a "home-field" advantage, a restaurant provides a neutral territory, but less privacy.

House Gifts

A house gift for the host is a kind gesture. It need not be fancy or expensive. Everyone has different tastes, and a perfect gift is not possible. In my opinion, the best gift does not become an imposing or permanent fixture (e.g., a gigantic vase or an oil painting of dogs playing poker). Fruit baskets are generally safe. Cut flowers or a potted plant would be fine as well. Home-cooked specialty items such as desserts can add a personal touch. Ultimately, it is the thought that counts.

A bottle of wine is a perfectly common and acceptable house gift for American households, but not necessarily Indian ones. As orthodoxy among Indian people varies, it is better to err on the side of caution.

Other Orthodoxy

If applicable, considering orthodoxy in other matters is also appropriate. For example, some Indian households in the U.S. object to wearing footwear indoors, but others do not. Simply follow the host's example. Anticipating potential awkwardness, socks should be presentable and not outrageous in style (e.g., without holes, emblems of cartoon characters, or rainbow colors with individual compartments for each toe).

Orthodoxy in a diet is also potential issue. For example, not all Indians eat meat, and not all Brahmins eat onions and garlic. Cooking wine in a sauce may offend some strict teetotalers. Some observant Indians serve rice only at engagements or weddings, not at an initial ensemble meeting.

It is considerate to ask in advance about any dietary requirements. Dining-in places that responsibility on the host. Dining-out places that responsibility on the restaurant. It is safer to choose a place with a wide menu. For example, a vegetarian menu would suit vegetarians and non-vegetarians. Thankfully, vegetarian food can be flavorful enough that most non-vegetarians do not "miss" meat. If necessary, truly dedicated carnivores can pick up buffalo wings on the ride home.

The Flow of Conversation

At an ensemble meeting, actual introductions may be in order, even if the identities are obvious. Often, people know who is who in advance, but a formal introduction is polite. Having some previous contact helps the flow of conversation. Typically, everyone sits in the same room, and the discussion is general. Side conversations can be okay, as long as they do not disrupt the overall group. The shy may contribute less because of the group's size. With fewer people, each should contribute more.

Although it is an artificial circumstance, it need not stay that way. If the atmosphere is inviting, conversation can flow without much difficulty. People skilled at small talk have no problem. If there is reasonable interest, the conversation will flow. Extreme reluctance and displeasure can be evident if the boy or girl looks totally disgusted and unhappy. Detecting this displeasure does not require formal training in psychiatry.

Comparable to advice in attending an interview, all people should be themselves. Yes, a good first impression is desirable, but one should not try too hard. Avoid what Southerners in the U.S. term "putting on airs," and the British term "getting above oneself." Especially, the young people should not pretend to be someone they are not. If a relationship evolves from this meeting, each person should feel comfortable with him or herself in the other's company, not some inaccurate perception.

False Advertising

By design, an ensemble meeting involves coordinating several schedules. Traveling to the meeting costs money and time for everyone. For all these reasons, any significant change or potential problem should be conveyed to the appropriate people as soon as possible.

In my case, I was on-call at the ensemble meeting when I met the woman who later became my wife. I communicated this problem immediately and could not change the on-call date. Luckily, it turned out that I had to excuse myself only a few times to answer the pager.

An ensemble meeting should contain the major and willing participants. If some are absent or unwilling, it is appropriate to have a full disclosure of the probable participants at the meeting. An ensemble meeting may not be entirely productive. It may be best to proceed in another way or abandon the idea altogether. This way, there is no false advertising or wasted time or money.

My wife had a more disturbing tale. Soon before an earlier ensemble meeting, her mother called the potential sambandhi who only then informed her that the actual varan would be absent. An ensemble meeting without the man of the hour seemed pointless, but it was too late to cancel the tickets. They learned later the varan was actually in India on a mission to find a wife. His mother did not bother informing the guests of this minor detail.

Outcomes of the Ensemble Meeting: Positive and Fair

After the ensemble meeting, it is a nice touch to write a thank-you letter or card, not just a phone call. The guest could thank the host for hospitality, or the host could thank the guest for coming. The boy or girl could certainly write this letter, but its coming from a parent is more formal. Even if the ensemble meeting went poorly, a follow-up "thank you" is still a polite recognition.

An ensemble meeting that went well will prompt the couple to meet again, obviously. Even if it went just "okay," one possibility is for the couple to give it a chance. The boy and girl can talk individually afterward and see how it goes. Going on a few dates may clarify the situation. The next chapter describes the shift from an ensemble meeting to an individual date.

Follow-up and Closure

A disastrous ensemble meeting may be the first and last time that this group gathers. Some circumstances may be inexcusable and justify discontinuing all further contact. I heard of one ensemble meeting that featured a rude and arrogant host family that seemed more interested in humiliating their guests than anything else.

Even if an ensemble meeting went poorly, it is polite to provide closure with a tactful follow-up letter or phone call. It did require some effort expended from all parties. A clear decision is preferable to fading into the sunset without a word.

Chapter 12

The First Date: Ideas and Etiquette

"The meeting of two persons is like the contact of two chemical substances. If there is any reaction, both are transformed."

Carl Jung

An actual date should involve only two people, or it is not a "date" per se. Actually, I know a man who went on his so-called honeymoon with his new parents-in-law who argued that they had always wanted to visit the newlyweds' destination. What better time than now? Withering logic prevailed.

Many different paths lead to the common endpoint of a date between a boy and girl. Given the differences in the paths, it is worth considering the features of each path first. Then we can consider the common features of a date.

Long Distance

The small pool of single Indians does not disqualify a varan or varani who is some distance away. Immediately taking on a long trip to see such a person is unlikely and inadvisable. The typical course is more gradual, beginning with a few conversations on the phone usually. Over time, the couple can determine if they would like to meet directly. Greater distances require more careful considerations. It would be a waste to travel a long distance to meet someone who seemed barely okay on the phone. However, it would be less of an effort to see the same person locally.

The couple must consider some obvious logistical considerations in order to meet. They must determine a suitable weekend or holiday when both are available. Where to meet depends on geography and personality. If a great distance separates the two, meeting in the middle is an option. If one person is in Los Angeles and the other in Washington, DC, meeting in St. Louis is a compromise. For the purposes of this discussion, this type of meeting will be termed "neutral territory" and elaborated below.

Alternatively, one person's location can be nominated as a possible host city, if both are comfortable with that idea. In this case, the Los Angelino would travel to the nation's capital to see the Washingtonian, or vice versa. There is no clear rule if the boy or girl should serve as host. Some specific issues about this situation are discussed below.

Driving Distance

As mentioned above, often a vast range qualifies as "driving distance" for many Indians. My wife believes that her father has made long enough road trips to qualify as a Teamster and receive truckers' benefits. "Long distance" here is defined as requiring more time driving to and from the destination than the time spent there.

On a date, driving is easier than flying. If a road trip is possible, the boy and girl usually consider earlier on the possibility of meeting for a date. One person could drive to the other's town, or a compromise is to meet between the two locations.

Safety

Through preliminary exchanges, each person has formed a general impression of the other. If it goes well, this impression is positive. At a minimum, each should feel that the other is decent. Indeed, why interact with indecent people unless necessary? Plenty of indecency exists without seeking it actively.

Often Indians believe that merely being Indian provides for some decency. With this belief, it seems perfectly okay to travel some distance to meet a virtual stranger who may become one's future spouse. Most Indians will not find totally peculiar the structure or the idea of this trip. Spending the night at that person's place seems fine as well. After all, the other person is also Indian.

What could go wrong?

Plenty.

Believing in the innate goodness of Indians could be harmful or even dangerous, as elaborated below. Most importantly, this belief is not true. Indians are not uniformly decent toward other Indians. Attending a large Indian function or boarding a flight to India should eliminate this fantasy. Plenty of *indecency* exists. No group, including Indians, has cornered the market on virtue. The same is true for vice.

Neutral Territory

As mentioned above, neutral territory can be safer than one person's residence. Knowing some other people in that neutral territory can make this option even more attractive. A friend or relative could provide not only room and board, but also a sense of safety to their visitor. This would be different than traveling to neutral territory in the middle of nowhere without a personal connection.

One disadvantage to staying with someone in neutral territory is decreased privacy. The purpose of the trip is an obvious question, "So why are you here to visit us and where do you need to go for four hours on a Saturday night?" The guest may or may not feel comfortable disclosing the reason for the visit. Alternatively, it could be advertised as meeting a "friend."

Get a Room or Two

As gentleman-like behavior or a sexist double standard, the stakes are probably different for men and women. A woman housing an overnight varan in her place may be different than a man housing a varani. If the boy and girl cannot easily return to their individual residences after the date, it is worth considering a hotel room.

It is important to talk openly about this issue. The host's residence may not easily accommodate an overnight guest, and privacy is compromised. There is no harm in stating all of this plainly. Without requiring an explanation, each person should respect the other's safety and privacy. The guest would be taking the host for granted in assuming that hotel rooms are unnecessary. The privacy and safety provided by the hotel can be worth it for both parties.

The host should not endure extreme hardship in housing the guest. Indians are generally hospitable folks. However, the Indian enthusiasm and ability in accommodating make-shift sleeping arrangements can be extraordinary. Akin to harboring fugitives, I personally hosted five adults and one teenager for a week-end in a tiny one-bedroom dormer apartment with one bathroom. Protests regarding overall comfort were dismissed as fussy, un-Indian, or not social. I was countered with tall tales of even worse circumstances endured previously (e.g., "I attended a wedding in Thanjavur in 1964 that makes this arrangement look luxurious!"). It is one matter to host known guests as I did, but it would have been totally unacceptable if a varani were involved.

If the meeting is in neutral territory, two hotel rooms should be considered. Obviously, staying at the same hotel would not be as safe. An ultra-cautious approach is to stay at different hotels, meet in a previously determined place, and not disclose the location of each person's hotel.

Case Study and Lessons Learned

An example would be helpful. A young Indian woman, "Devi," became acquainted with a varan, "Mahesh," through some phone calls. They decided to meet for a weekend, and they agreed that she would stay in a separate bedroom at his place. Devi traveled by plane a few hours to Mahesh's city. After he picked her up at the airport, she wished that she had asked about his driving record. His careless driving style seemed suicidal and homicidal. He seemed sober, but he drove drunk.

After that reminder of mortality, Mahesh recommended watching a movie. Devi agreed to see anything except the latest James Bond movie, which she had seen only recently. They went to see the latest James Bond movie. On the ride home, the neighborhood roads became a high-speed slalom course, as Mahesh swerved to avoid speed bumps. Closer to dinner, he asked her preferences in restaurants. She agreed to anything except Mexican food, which she had numerous times the previous week. They went to Mexican food.

Back at his place, Mahesh concluded openly that he considered himself a good catch. Then, he made some minor physical advances on Devi, but she stood up quickly to prevent anything further. Announcing that she was tired, she quickly escaped to her designated bedroom and locked the door immediately. She shuddered at what she faced: staying overnight in the home of a recklessly driving, pompous, selfish, creepy stranger in a town where she knew no one else. Back home the next day, Devi's parents were alarmed that this weekend away reduced their daughter to a shell of her former self.

Some features of the weekend were easily avoidable and fixable, and other others were not. Legally mandated programs could have improved Mahesh's driving. Classes on listening skills could have benefited him. He could have learned to keep his hands to himself. Psychotherapy could have addressed his narcissism. All of these projects are long-term.

In the short-term, however, Devi could have spoken to Mahesh a few more times to see if the long trip was worth it. They could have met in neutral territory. If possible, each person could have stayed with a relative or a friend there. If not possible, two separate rooms at the same hotel would have been an alternative. Staying at different hotels would be even safer. It would have been safer for each person to rent a car.

Even if Mahesh wanted to host her in his town, Devi could have rented a car and ensure a potential means of escape. In addition to offering a separate bedroom at his place, Mahesh could have suggested a reservation at a nearby hotel, if she would prefer. To be extra nice, he could have even offered to pay for it. Alternatively, he could have asked Devi if she would prefer to increase her privacy in making her own reservation. All these measures would not have guaranteed a perfect weekend, but it would have decreased the trauma.

"First Date" Defined

For the purposes of this discussion, a "date" here refers to a meeting of two people that spans some hours and ends with each going to separate places. This differs from ensemble meetings discussed earlier and two people spending a full weekend together, as mentioned above.

When

After confirming mutual interest in a date, the next step is to determine when to meet. For first dates, meeting for lunch is a good option. Compared to dinner, lunch tends to be more relaxed and less formal. After a good lunch date, it is easy to do something else such as going to a café or taking a stroll. A *really* good lunch date may become a dinner date as well. On the other hand, a disastrous lunch date does not ruin the whole day. A corrective emotional experience with a friend is still possible.

What

Dining together is a perfectly fine idea for a first date. A related question is if the couple will dine in or out. Dining in provides a more personal touch, assuming that the host can cook. As described in ensemble meetings, the host can ask the guest about any dietary requirements, aversions, and preferences. However, restaurants typically have an increased variety of food. Lapses in conversation are not so obvious. It is safer to be in a public place than a private residence.

How

Apart from determining a time, the couple should determine how to meet. Obviously, this will be determined by schedules, location, and transportation. Gentleman-like behavior dictates that the boy pick up the girl. Safety dictates the exact opposite: the girl uses her own means of transportation to meet the boy. For practical reasons or safety, the couple may choose to meet at a certain place. It is best to choose an easily accessible and uncrowded place such as the entrance to a café or restaurant. Statues can be a useful meeting point. On blind dates, it is helpful to provide some accurate and objective self-description. Designating particular clothing can be helpful (e.g., "I'll wear an orange construction worker's jacket and matching hard hat.").

Here is an example of how *not* to proceed. My wife once somehow decided to meet a so-so varan. They intended to "meet" at a ski area. Neither designated when and where exactly they would meet. Rightfully, she thought that the ski area would have only a limited number of Indian skiers and snowboarders. Indian boy could easily spot Indian girl, presumably. My wife helpfully added that her ski cap has a cartoon logo on it. Not surprisingly, she did not meet the varan that day, but she enjoyed skiing, and he may have also.

Where and Interferences

Ultimately, the forum of the date should foster two people spending time together and becoming more familiar with each other. By implication, anything interfering with that process should be avoided. A date at a deafening dance club is not conducive to conversation, for example. The "conversation" is actually yelling brief statements in each other's ear.

Dining together is generally a safe bet. Everyone eats. A full mouth should disqualify conversation, but chatting before or after chewing is fine. "Dinner plus a movie" is a popular, but curiously standard date. Dining before the movie requires eating against a deadline to catch the movie. A movie theater is not conducive to conversation in the moment. At least, it should not be. Dining after a movie may offer fewer choices of restaurants, if it is late.

The first date should not involve differing levels of talent or a formal score. For example, a guy offered to take out a friend of mine to play golf at an exclusive country club. Even if the surroundings were magnificent, varying skill and scores demonstrated the better golfer. This outing would be more suitable in a more mature relationship, but no first date should involve competitive sports.

If it must occur at all, keeping score on a date should be an informal process (e.g., points gained for good manners). Sure, people can eat competitively. Personally, I regret that a former colleague of mine and I did not actually have an eating contest at all-you-can-eat salad bar, as we had long discussed. However, this idea would not be so common for a first date.

A date can be adversely affected by different tastes. Early on, each does not know another person's preferences. It works well to do something mutually interesting and appealing. A date at an exclusive seafood restaurant would be unsuitable for those who experience life-threatening allergies to shellfish. Discuss where to go and what to do.

Artistic tastes or lack thereof may be unknown initially. Insisting on a specialized jazz concert for a first date may be gratifying for a passionate fan who cannot understand how anyone could dislike this music. The concert would be awkward. Of course, this concert would be perfectly fine if the couple has a common interest in jazz.

Dancing, amusement parks, mountaineering, gladiator sports, marathons, monster truck rallies, and hunting are all best postponed.

Preparation and Meeting Up

In an era of plenty, the perennial question is, "What to wear?" Attention to appearance is part of a good impression. Long hours at a salon and fussing are unnecessary. It is appropriate to cover the two fundamentals: take a shower and wear ironed clothes. If the date involves traveling to another town, these two fundamentals are still applicable. Allow enough travel time to shower and dress before the date. Wrinkles in clothes can be reduced by keeping each garment in the individual plastic bag provided by dry cleaners.

If there is any question, it is better to dress up than dress down. Women have more freedom in clothing and can find something "nice" and comfortable. Men should wear collared shirts. If it suits the man, an established pattern of facial hair is fine. Goatees and Vandykes are currently popular. However, facial hair should not be in transition on a first date (e.g., a 3-day old goatee). The same is true for women.

A friend of mine once met a guy for coffee as a very informal blind date. Although she wore neat and casual clothing, she wondered if she should have bothered. Her date wore an old t-shirt, wrinkled cotton shorts, and worn sandals. Her inescapable impression was that she made some effort, but he did not.

Phone Numbers and Cell Phones

If meeting at some public place, it is helpful for both people to have the telephone number of the meeting point such as a restaurant. If applicable, the one with the home-field advantage can provide that telephone number. Even if it is obtainable through directory assistance or the Internet, it takes just a few minutes to look up that number and let the visitor know. Each person can then call the meeting point for detailed and relevant directions. People at the meeting point commonly field this question and typically provide the best instructions.

Additionally, exchanging cellular telephone numbers is useful as well. Of course, each person should remember to keep the phone charged and turned on. Any last-minute problems can be easily conveyed via cellular phone. Two counter examples can be illustrative.

For a first date, I sorely underestimated rush hour traffic and a terrible storm of biblical proportions. I was delayed by 15 minutes. My date—who later became my wife—later confessed that she misinterpreted my late arrival. She wondered if I would stand her up.

I detest the unquestionably dangerous practice of driving while talking on a cell phone. However, it would have been safe and easy for me to make a quick call while literally parked on the expressway. One central problem was that I did not own a cell phone back then.

A second example is more distressing. One young woman known to me, "Archana," agreed to meet a varan, "Ramesh," for dinner at a restaurant. When Archana left for the date, she had general directions and Ramesh's cell phone number, but not the restaurant's number. When she became totally lost, a gas station attendant provided her with some vague directions, leading her to think that she was not that far away.

When Archana called Ramesh's cell phone, she could only leave a message on his voice mail. This scenario was repeated three times, but once she broke through. When she finally arrived, she found that he had finished most of his dinner. Her extreme hunger prompted her to eat while he watched. This was the first and last time that the two met.

This unpleasant date provides at least three lessons. First, calling the restaurant directly can be helpful in obtaining directions, and it is helpful to keep the telephone number for the date itself. Again, the restaurant staff can most likely help a lost customer. Second, cell phones are helpful only if they are turned on. Third, reading while waiting is more polite than eating most of the meal alone.

The Date Itself

Once both people have arrived safely at their destination, the date itself can begin. As recommended earlier, be yourself. Shake hands when saying hello. Of course, feeling nervous or an occasional loss for words is common. Most likely, nervousness decreases with time, especially when discussing familiar topics and shared interests. Maintain eye contact. Be nice and polite.

Dining Etiquette

The popularity of dining on a date requires some particular comments on this process. While proceeding toward the table, offer to your date the seat with a better view. For example, it is usually more pleasant to look out a window than at a wall. Determining the better seat is partly based on intuition and does not require studying *Vasthu Sasthram* or *Feng Shui*.

Soft drinks are obviously the safest bet. Caffeine can increase anxiety in the susceptible. Choose accordingly. Alcohol in moderation is fine. Do not choose an extremely expensive bottle of wine. Obviously, becoming totally drunk on the first date does not create a good impression. It also can lead to bad judgment. Do not drive drunk. It is less polite to start eating while the other person is still awaiting food.

The Bill

By history, gallantry dictates that the boy pays the entire bill. The reformed approach is to split the bill, or "going Dutch." Even in these enlightened times, the issue of who pays the bill remains controversial.

Money has symbolic and representational value. The girl may feel indebted toward the boy who pays the entire bill. The central question is what he expects in return, if anything. A friend of mine went on a horrible, but expensive, date wherein the guy paid in full. She felt obligated to resubject herself to the misery of his company so that she could pay the bill the next time. With the score evened, she could dump him with a clear conscience.

I heard of one guy who goes Dutch only if he has a platonic relationship with a woman. If the relationship is not platonic, he pays his companion's way entirely. Given such a lovely specimen, splitting the bill may remove that sense of indebtedness and the need to even the score.

On all first dates, I expected to pay the bill. If my date vehemently insisted, then we split the bill. In return for paying the bill in full, a simple acknowledgement of "thank you" was sufficient for me. Most of my dates were accordingly polite. One obnoxious exception was a varani who said nothing and simply pushed the bill toward me. I was prepared to pay the bill in full, but I found her move obnoxious.

On an early date, another friend of mine was asked out to the opera, which she enjoys somewhat. The high cost of the tickets made my friend feel awkward about accepting the offer, even if her date loved the opera. He argued that he would like to attend regardless, and he would enjoy her company at the performance. She appreciated his generosity in buying the opera ticket. However, she was not sure if she saw much of a future with him. Her quandary was wondering if attending the opera created an indebtedness toward him that would cause resentment if they did not meet again. A less expensive date may not have produced such awkwardness.

On one date, my wife gathered that the varan made ten times her salary. When the bill came, he immediately suggested that they go Dutch. She could certainly afford her share, but his lack of generosity astonished her. They did not meet again. She also did not care for his white tube socks.

Chapter 13

Evolving a Relationship

The first date should determine the answer to one obvious question—will there be a second date? In the happiest circumstance, the answer is clearly "yes." One step removed from this is "maybe." At the other extreme is "no." Admittedly, it is usually easier to decide if a second date is not desirable. For example, the worst date of my life reminded me of a short review of a performance about twenty years ago. That review stated the program began promptly at 8 PM. At midnight, the critic looked at his watch, but it displayed only 8:15 PM.

My date was terrible, because we had so little in common. I did not feel inclined to work too hard to carry on the conversation that so frequently trailed off. My overall impression was that she only wanted to get this date over with. At my perceived "midnight," I offered to drive her home, and I was relieved that she accepted. Perhaps she felt the same way.

Although this date ended on neutral terms, I was not interested in another date with her, and I suspect that the feeling was mutual. I doubt that either of us had pillows damp with tears about not meeting again. That date was only a few hours in my life and hers, and no serious or irreparable damage occurred. Neither the police nor the emergency department was involved. In that way, if this date is my worst, I should consider myself fortunate.

Really good and really bad dates produce clear decisions. Rejections and related matters are discussed further in the next chapter. Let's begin with a more positive outcome of a favorable first encounter.

Making Time to Date

Assume that a first date has proceeded well and more dates follow. Repeated contact allows each person to form a fuller impression of the other. Ideally, this fuller impression is also favorable and positive. Clearly, it would be disappointing to discover that the favorable first impression was an accident.

If the first date went well, the next phase requires continuing that interest and maintaining momentum. In fact, mere exposure to someone increases the chances of liking that person, as demonstrated in a classic study by Saegert and colleagues (1973). By definition, all of this requires some work. Talking on the phone requires time and some effort. Going on a date also requires some time, effort, and money. All of this is possible only if both feel that this endeavor is worthwhile. If dating is a sufficient priority, people will make time to date. Not making time may reflect the following: playing games with calling, a temporary situation, lack of interest, or a personality trait. Consider each feature in turn:

Playing Games with Calling

Whatever the backdrop, the telephone is a convenient and common means of establishing and maintaining contact. Obviously, calling after a date is certainly appropriate and necessary if the two wish to remain in contact. Plenty of thoughts, advice, and badmouthing exist on the whole issue of phone calls. Deciding whether to call or wait for a call is one fundamental question. For coy reasons, the answer to this question may be independent of actual interest (e.g., "The date was fun, but that person needs to call me."). The decision may be fueled by not wanting to appear too forward, desperate, or uncool.

If the person has decided to call, the next question is when to call. Here also, plenty of deliberation may occur. Finding the right time on the right day may be intensely considered. For some, this borders on determining an auspicious astrological time. Some practical considerations, such as a late night at work, may also surface.

Strong thoughts about who should call whom may also enter the picture. The timing of the phone call can be subject to a psychological interpretation (e.g., "Calling on the second Wednesday of the month means insufficient interest."). On top of all of this, friends and relatives can offer their welcome and unwelcome opinions (e.g., "Picking up on the first ring means desperation.").

There is no need to complicate or overthink matters. If you are agreed to call during the week, then call during the week. If you are interested, make the call. Even if you are "busy," it takes only a few minutes to leave a message during the day on a home answering machine. Indicate when you are available or when you will try again. If the person calls back, great. If not, consider trying again. If still no response, take a hint.

Temporary Situation

A relationship may originate at an awkward time. Of course, a leisurely time would be better, but that does not always occur. For example, boy meets girl, and they hit it off well on the first date. Soon thereafter, the boy's dear grandparent dies suddenly, and he must travel to spend time with his family. The circumstances of death were beyond anyone's control. At least, they should be. Assuming no foul play, the boy returns home after spending time with his family, but acute grief prevents normal life from resuming immediately.

Even if the boy had a splendid date just before his grandparent's death, he is understandably not in his best form afterward. However, time should allow him to return to his usual self. This is one example of a temporary situation. Early on, the boy and girl could simply talk about how to proceed (e.g. who will contact whom and when).

Once, my temporary situation was a unique opportunity to travel abroad for a few weeks with a good friend to visit his country of origin. I mentioned this opportunity to the varani whom I had been seeing casually. At the time, it would have been awkward for us to travel together internationally. Given my love of travel, I went ahead on the trip that proved to be one of the best of my life. Soon after I returned, however, the varani broke up with me.

Another friend of mine offered a different explanation to my story. Based on his similar experience, he concluded that travel south of the Tropic of Cancer spells peril for any relationship. After such a trip, he returned home to find that his girlfriend had broken up with him and cleaned out his place thoroughly. He claimed that it resembled a looted city during a power failure. Fortunately, my friend did not sound as embittered as Ike Turner, and he treated his "Tina" much better.

Lack of Interest

Not making time to date may simply reflect a lack of interest in dating as an idea or in seeing a particular person. Despite lacking interest, these dedicated singles know people who harass them into a blind date or another arrangement. Again, married people and members of a cult like to recruit others into the fold. The single person may be willing to try one date without jumping into the cult totally. Certainly, the single person's possible misgivings would be set aside if the date proceeds well. On the other hand, lack of interest may be evident on an unpleasant date. An eager follow-up phone call is unlikely.

Personality

Some are not fully interested in dating because of their personality—and lack thereof, I daresay. The pace of life is intense for most young people. Hours at work are long. Time-consuming ambitions to climb the business ladder may exist. Little else remains.

Although it may reflect reality, being "busy" is an excuse for everyone. However, its validity extends only so far. One friend of mine works ridiculously long hours and travels extensively for work. Although he is certainly busy, he disapproves of this as an excuse. My friend may apologize for a delayed response, but he thinks that "busy" is a cop out.

Even if one is truly busy, it takes just a few seconds to make a call during the day to leave a message on an answering machine. This does not take the place of an actual conversation, obviously. However, it can help demonstrate some ongoing interest and future availability. Some exchanges of phone tag could set a good time to talk.

There may also be a sense that there is plenty of time to marry later on. Right now, being single and unattached may suit the person well. A sense of conflict about dating and marriage may also exist. For one reason or a variety, the person cannot or does not take the time to date.

Some personal habits and tendencies may also play a role. Being overly hurried and on the move does not favor making the time to date leisurely. Disorganization causes lost telephone numbers and details. There may be some interest, but this kind of behavior causes the other person to form an inaccurate perception of the situation.

Along these lines, once I had a discussion with an interesting varani, "Tara," who seemed unprepared for my call and uncertain about the Indian matrimonial process. We chatted a bit, just the same. Given her ambivalence, I provided Tara my telephone number at the end of the conversation and asked her to call me if she wished. I was disinclined to sell her further on the general idea of the Indian matrimonial process plus the specific possibility of going out with me.

All of the sudden, Tara called me a long time afterward. In the interim, she had decided clearly that she wanted to marry an Indian. Evidently, our individual conversation played a role in Tara's thoughts and decision. She had recently rediscovered my number that she had "misplaced." She wondered what ever became of that less-than-totally ridiculous Indian boy who called her a while ago. As it turned out, I had recently become engaged to someone else. Tara graciously congratulated me and half thought that this may have happened.

Second and Subsequent Dates

Assuming that both people have made dating a priority, they may start viewing their situation in a different light. Dating now becomes spending time with an increasingly familiar person. The comfort and ease of interaction should also increase. If all is going well, the two people may start viewing themselves as a couple and look forward to their next date.

As mentioned in the previous chapter, the setting for the first date should be conducive to conversation. The same is essentially true for subsequent dates.

Spectator golf and observing chess matches interfere with each person from becoming more familiar with the other.

What the couple does on a date may also change. Dinner at home may replace one at a formal restaurant. Spending time at one person's place leisurely may be more common than a planned activity. The couple may watch a movie at home rather than in a theater. Regardless of venue, the aim is for the couple to become better acquainted.

Boundaries

As mentioned earlier, casual relationships in the West may not be disclosed to the family. This contrasts the Indian approach of families knowing about the relationship since its immature origins.

As the relationship between boy and girl is proceeding, parents and others may be eager for progress reports. After all, they may have played a role in its creation. So why should they not play a role in its maintenance? Alternatively, why is the relationship not progressing?

The answer to all these questions rests in the issue of boundaries. As described earlier, boundaries in psychiatry relate to conforming to appropriate and defined roles. Good boundaries dictate that a psychiatrist and a patient meet only in the office. The psychiatrist is not the patient's bartender, taxi driver, or priest. By the psychiatrist's remaining within an appropriate role as a psychiatrist, the patient stands the best chance of improvement.

Maintaining good boundaries allows a psychotherapeutic relationship, or one between parent and child, to mature and flourish. The parent should not be an interrogator, complete confidante, or chum. Of course, some aspects of those roles may be present even in healthy parent-child relationships. Nevertheless, the child's relationship is most likely to flourish if the parent remains primarily a parent.

Parents who have introduced their offspring to a varan or varani have provided an introduction. The remaining and most difficult part is up to the young couple. It is entirely up to them how they get along, when they meet, what they discuss, and so on. Of course, natural curiosity and an interest in seeing their children married may compel Indian parents to be more curious and persistent. However, all of that is appropriate only up to a point.

Type of Residence

Many eligible Indian singles live on their own. However, a fair number may live with others. For economic and social reasons, having a roommate may be a good idea. For various reasons, including loyalty, a person may live with family.

Whatever the motivation, the type of residence can play a role in how this person dates. The main issue concerns privacy. Even if others are temporarily dismissed from the residence, dating someone who lives with others is different than dating someone who lives alone.

In my case, I lived in a house with two other people during my training. This in turn influenced my thoughts on what to do on a date. While living alone, I would have invited my local date to dinner at my place. However, this would not have been as easy to do with two housemates. One was never home, and the obsessive one was home too often. If I really wanted, I could have asked these two to leave during my private dinner. However, that would not have been entirely reasonable or fair.

I am still not sure what to make of one varani who had a confusing number of housemates, but her parents and I remained ignorant of the exact figure and composition. For all I know, she was running an informal shelter without a license.

Introduction to Friends

Through courtship, each member of the couple can meet the other's friends. We cannot choose our family, but we can choose our friends. There is wisdom in the expression of being judged by the company that we keep. Our friends do say something about ourselves.

Before my wife and I were engaged, we had dinner with two former colleagues of mine who were interested to meet her. One colleague's wife insisted on referring to my date as my "fiancée." When I argued that I had no fiancée at the time, I heard the wise prediction that I would soon.

A related issue is exactly which friends to introduce. It can be a pleasure for a significant other to meet some friends. At the same time, it is no accident that I met some questionable friends of my wife only after we were engaged. She was concerned that an earlier introduction would cause me to head for the hills. In fact, she believed that my departure would be entirely justified. Similarly, it is also no accident that only after we married, I introduced her to some characters known to me. Her fleeing would have also demonstrated good judgment.

Obviously, a scheduled meeting is different than encountering someone unintentionally. It is a small world and such chance encounters are possible in many places. Before we were engaged, my wife and I were in a supermarket near my parents' house. We ran into and briefly said hello to an uncle known to my parents. Avoiding him seemed inappropriate and unnecessary. He seemed pleased to see me and appreciated the introduction to my companion. To the best of my knowledge, he did not rent a billboard in town announcing whom he had seen next to frozen vegetables earlier. Later, he saw me individually and commented simply, "She seems nice."

Contacts with Family

The stakes are a bit different in introducing a varan or varani to the family, if an ensemble meeting did not occur earlier. Even if an ensemble meeting occurred, Indian parents typically have an open policy that the varan or varani is welcome at their place at any time. In fact, home-cooked food may be held as an incentive to visit, especially if the food has regional attraction (e.g., *dosai, appam, samosa*).

Premarital Sex

Historically, the marriage ceremony usually occurred prior to puberty, and the couple started living together only later. All sexual awakenings and related interests were directed at one already designated person: the spouse. Since the ban of child marriages in India, the typical expectation was that sex would be postponed until marriage. Most Indian parents in the U.S. retain this line of thinking.

Ulterior Question

Along the way, there still remains one ulterior question: can the couple imagine a future together? Casual relationships with a platonic or uncertain future are not the norm in the Indian context. Of course, such relationships are possible, but they are not common. Typically, a resolution is required. Will the platonic relationship progress beyond friendship or not? Can the uncertainty of the relationship be resolved? If the answer to either question is "no," typically the couple breaks up.

The large issue of rejections is considered in the next chapter.

Chapter 14

Rejections and Break-ups: Tactful, Tactless, Reasonable, and Unreasonable

The previous chapter described relationships that are going well. Subsequent chapters will consider relationships going even better and proceeding toward a commitment. Before the conclusion of living happily ever after, however, it is worthwhile to consider the relationships that do not end that way.

Obviously, everyone is not intended for everyone else. If this were true, this book would be unnecessary. However, there is usually someone for everyone. Nice people often find nice people. Shallow people find shallow people. Sexy people find sexy people. Smart people find smart people. And so on.

At least one old study supports this notion. Walster and colleagues (1978) outlined an equity theory that people cannot expect more in relationships than what they themselves have to offer. Perhaps the increased level of entitlement in society has not refuted that theory since 1978.

Most people do not marry the first person that they ever dated. I did not. For this reason, it is necessary to consider the issue of breaking a relationship, which will be termed "rejection" here.

Decency

The uneven distribution of grace and manners in society can be particularly evident in rejections. The graceful and well-mannered deliver the message tactfully through whatever means. The graceless and ill-mannered are less effective or simply offensive in delivering the same news. It is crucial to remember that the rejection can be a blow, even if the contact were minimal or casual. Also, a tactful rejection helps soften that blow on potentially fragile emotions. As elaborated below, politely conveying a rejection increases the chances of acceptance. Other rejections are weighed down in vagueness, bent realities, negligence, or rudeness.

Overview of Attraction

As mentioned in the Introduction, my declaring candidacy began around the time that my friend Kamal was aware of one varani who is a former model. Never mind that no fashion house ever pleaded with *me* to model their garments. Sour grapes aside, I probably have little in common with models.

Heads do not turn as I walk by. Why should I expect to be with people only of that caliber? This idea also has some foundation in the literature. Buunk (1996) described a matching theory that postulates that people tend to have partners at a similar level of attractiveness.

There is a distinction between beauty and attraction. Beautiful people are endowed with physically striking features in their appearance. Everyone agrees that they are gorgeous, very handsome, or stunning. By contrast, attractive people may have some positive physical features, but not necessarily as many as the truly beautiful. Attractive people engage others with some additional qualities such as poise, lively nature, sense of humor, or fashion sense.

Attraction is also different than infatuation. Being head over heels for someone is invigorating and exceeds simple attraction. Infatuation refers to an immature and temporary state of feeling. The question is whether the infatuation for a particular person can continue indefinitely or turn into more mature feelings.

Attraction is more subjective than beauty. Others can see the draw of a truly handsome man or beautiful woman. However, the draw of an attractive person may be totally unique and not so obvious. At times, the couple's mutual attraction is blatant. Two people can be happily matched overall, even if they appear mismatched in some other way. At other times, the question seems to be, "What does X see in Y?"

At some level, both members of the couple should feel attracted to each other for the relationship to proceed well. It should arise spontaneously, not in a forced or exaggerated way. The attraction may not be immediate or at first sight. Nevertheless, a mutual attraction should occur at some point for the couple.

Men and women have different views on the matter. Across 37 cultures, Buss and colleagues (1989) found that men more than women valued physical attractiveness in a mate, independent of the culture's economic development and wealth.

Grounds for Rejection: No Attraction

If there is no attraction at first, the difficult question then becomes if that attraction will ever occur. Time may help answer this question. At the same time, it is not always easy to identify or admit the lack of attraction to a person who has plenty of fine qualities. It is even more difficult to end such a relationship. However, delaying such an inevitable breakup benefits no one.

In my own experience, I have proceeded in such a relationship to see if time would help. It did not. I have also had the unsettling thought of wondering why I was not attracted to this very pleasant varani sitting across the way from me. She was very nice. We were having a decent time. She had many good qualities. We had enough in common to talk about. Why was I not attracted to her?

Postponing the end of the relationship would not make it any easier. I did not intend any breakup to reflect that she was not "good enough" for me. Rather, it returned to my idea that not everyone is intended for everyone else. Some women have determined that I was not for them. Similarly, some women were not for me. Breaking up merely reflects that difference.

Disclosing the reasons for the breakup is an entirely different matter and discussed further below.

Grounds for Rejection: Different Priorities

Through dating, each person forms a sense of what the other is like. Does one person prefer quiet evenings at home playing checkers and dominoes? Does another person have a long police record owing to wild nights on the town? Does one person like only fast food? Does the other feel content only at high-end restaurants where strategic bribes are necessary to secure the correct table? Does one person drop everything for family, while the other can vaguely recall the names of siblings?

These admittedly exaggerated descriptions demonstrate differences in behavior and preferences which are important in uniting or repelling two people. Successful relationships feature people with similar, not dissimilar, interests and personalities. Specifically, Werner (1979) in one study found that attraction was directly linked to similar preferences in leisure activities. The conclusion was that, "Those who play together stay together."

More generally, research has not supported the idea that "opposites attract." In an old study by Byrne (1971), sense of attraction was directly proportional to the number of attitudes that the couple held in common. People with vastly different priorities may not have enough common ground to maintain a relationship. A breakup may ensue.

Grounds for Rejection: Geography

In casual relationships, the idea of marriage develops only along the way, if at all. Agreeing to the Indian matrimonial process provides an implied approval of one outcome: marriage.

Whether formally or informally, the couple discusses marriage and related matters. One large issue is where to live. Some people have strong geographical requirements. Some Indian matrimonial advertisements directly state such loyalty (e.g., "must reside in greater New York"). Rather than a requirement, a preference for a city or region is less intense and more difficult to determine.

At times, it is easier to know where a person would *not* like to live. That is the case with my wife and me. We would not mind living in a number of places. Actually, she has fantasies about tropical locales, and I remain in the U.S. only on a tether.

Having a frank discussion about regional preferences is important. Clarifying each person's flexibility or inflexibility on this issue can save some grief. For a relationship to continue, both must accept any absolute requirement of living in only one region. If both do not accept this requirement, then attempting to create a relationship is pointless. Even though initial flexibility about regional preferences may not be sustained, discussing this topic early on is still worthwhile.

I know two relationships that turned sour because of regional preferences. In one example, "Deepa" accepted "Arun's" clear regional requirement. The couple married and lived in that required region. The marriage had some difficulties later, and Deepa wanted both of them to leave. Arun had always considered this issue fixed, and the idea of moving only worsened the situation. The marriage ended in divorce, and Deepa and Arun now live in their individually preferred regions.

In another example, "Jayanthi" had a geographical preference and was officially willing to consider moving. Jayanthi and "Krishna" discussed this issue and determined that geography would not prevent their marriage. Afterward, Jayanthi became extremely reluctant to move. The geographical preference turned into a requirement. Although the marriage was not terribly at risk in other ways, the change in Jayanthi's policy clearly had an impact.

Before marriage, Deepa and Arun plus Jayanthi and Krishna had discussed and evidently agreed on where they would like to live. However, it did not guarantee that they would live happily ever after. A successful outcome is not assured, but having the initial discussion is important nevertheless. As the old saying goes, it is better to try and fail rather than not try at all.

Grounds for Rejection: Kids

Another issue for discussion and possible difference of opinion is the issue of children. Here also, discussing the issue early on seems like putting the cart before the horse or the baby carriage before the pregnancy.

The historic expectation in India is that the married couple certainly will have children. In a traditional Hindu wedding, having children is cited as one desirable feature while walking around the holy fire seven times. As quoted in Erikson's *Gandhi's Truth* (1969), the Manusmriti states, "He is a perfect man who consists of three persons united: his wife, himself, and his offspring." Not having children was historically considered a severe absence, and similar sentiments are still present.

By implication, the Indian community abroad typically has valued married couples having children. However, some mainstream American couples do not wish to have children. This preference may also influence the generation of Indians raised in the U.S., even if it runs against tradition.

The desire or dislike of children obviously plays an important role in a marriage. Strong opinions pro- or con- can exist. Discussing such preferences early on can avoid future disappointment. Clearly, the easiest situations are both pro-baby or both con-baby. One pro- and one con-creates friction. Fierce arguments to overcome a strong opinion may not be entirely successful. It would be foolish to think one person can definitely change the other's opinion after marriage. If a strong opinion exists before marriage, it will likely continue after marriage.

If one person definitely wants a mob of kids, their creation requires cooperation from the spouse, obviously. At least, that is the direct, moral, and economical method. If only one spouse favors zero population growth, tension and bitter disappointment can follow.

Grounds for Rejection: Fading

Matters may be proceeding well enough for the couple to continue contact, but they may not be head over heels or working toward a commitment. If the relationship does not seem to be advancing beyond friendship, the couple can continue status quo by meeting up infrequently or casually. Alternatively, the relationship may lose momentum and fade away.

Fading away can be characterized by increased intervals of time between contact. Doing nothing may cause the relationship to dissolve totally. Reestablishing contact may restore positive momentum in the relationship. If these efforts are not recognized, take a hint. Do not follow the example of a professor at Waseda University in Japan. One woman declined his offer for a first date, and he called her back. He hung up on her without saying anything. He did this not just once, but 920 times, as reported in the *News of the Weird* (2002).

For a few years now, I am still awaiting a return phone call from a varani who told me that I was in her Rolodex. Since then, I have married and have children.

I believe that she is married as well. The chances of her calling me seem remote. For that matter, my telephone number has changed.

Grounds for Rejection: Dossier Only

After an exchange, one dossier may be returned to the sender with a rejection letter. The form and style of the rejection letter are totally open. Some can be tactfully worded, and others are hasty and tactless. The style matches the writer. In response to the rejection letter, returning a dossier may be appropriate. A cover letter may or may not be appropriate.

Once, my dossier was returned with a letter indicating that an astrologer discovered a *dhosham* or "flaw" in my horoscope that would spell doom for that particular varani. This letter enraged my father who replied that he would have accepted a general statement about astrological incompatibility. However, mentioning specific details about *dhosham* struck him as inappropriate and insulting. He wondered how that uncle would feel if a rejection letter stated that his daughter's dhosham is her horrendous appearance that makes dogs howl and babies cry.

A generally worded rejection letter is preferable to one that offers a flimsy excuse. Although I had no geographic requirement, one rejection letter stated that the varani did not want to move to my locale immediately. The so-called reason seemed devious.

Another time, my dossier was returned on the grounds that the varani "did not want to marry a psychiatrist," as best as could be determined from the scrawl in the letter. Before the dossiers were exchanged, my father confessed that his son is a psychiatrist. Either the varani's father was not paying attention, or the source of the rejection lies elsewhere.

Admittedly, not wanting to marry a psychiatrist may demonstrate sound judgment. My wife believes that psychiatrists ask too many questions.

Wording of the Rejection Letter

Even if there is a specific reason, it need not be conveyed. At the risk of sounding business-like, the rejection may be worded in a general way:

> *"Thank you for sending your child's materials. After careful consideration, we have decided that we are not interested in pursuing an alliance. We appreciate your interest and wish you well in your search."*

If the reason is not offensive, conveying it tactfully is acceptable:

> *"Based on the information that you provided, we consulted our astrologer in India who determined that the two horoscopes are not compatible. We regret that this is the case, as an alliance between our children seemed favorable initially."*

If the reason is potentially offensive, a generally worded rejection letter is much more tactful. Listing the specific reason benefits no one. The rejecting party can appear pompous or arrogant. The rejected party can feel insulted or angry.

Grounds for Rejection: Gut Feeling or Inner Voice

The chapter on cyberdating offered some recommendations about paying attention to a gut feeling or inner voice about relationships. Of course, this gut feeling can be true in a positive sense when a relationship is going well. At the same time, a gut feeling is also true in unfavorable or unsatisfying relationships. Fundamental doubts and discomfort about relationships should not be ignored. Their importance should be considered more closely. If desired, discussing matters with a trusted third party can be helpful.

The issue of fundamental doubt presented itself once to me. On vacation in India, my cousin's distant relative, Shanthi, wanted to talk to me, specifically because I am a psychiatrist. This is never a good sign. I vaguely remembered seeing Shanthi once in childhood, and I recall a Frisbee being present.

When she arrived, I told her upfront that I was off duty and not going to conduct a psychiatric examination. Indeed, I have never conducted one while unshaven and wearing Indian clothes. Although Shanthi accepted this, she wanted my opinion on how to proceed with some of her concerns regarding clinical depression. Basically, I heard her situation and recommended that she return to her local psychiatrist. That was the easy part.

The conversation then turned to her recent and hasty engagement to a varan who struck her as slippery. In addition to his indefinite financial status, Shanthi could not imagine growing fond of him or spending the rest of her life with him. All of this culminated in the obvious question of why she agreed to the engagement in the first place. One thing led to another, and she decided that evening to end the engagement with my cousin and aunt's help. I later learned that Shanthi was doing much better and became happily engaged to a much more suitable man.

Later, I confessed to my cousin that I had a blunt discussion with a friend of mine that partly contributed to his decision to end an incompatible engagement.

Not to be outdone, my cousin said that her frank discussions with two different colleagues contributed to their ending incompatible engagements.

In all these cases, some internal disquiet was ignored initially. Fortunately, the relationships ended before a potentially disastrous marriage. Paying attention to that sinking feeling would have been helpful in preventing misery.

In residency, I learned that one's taste in the arts is not random and reflects the unconscious. At that point, I had an epiphany about my course with an earlier varani. Namely, the two songs that remind me of my time with her are "Let It Go," by Prince and "Prayer for the Dying," by Seal. Paying closer attention to my unconscious would have made me realize that this relationship would not work.

Grounds for Rejection: Violence

A gut feeling or inner voice implies some features that cannot be pinpointed. Something is wrong, but identifying it clearly may not be easy or possible. The reasons may seem trivial (e.g., prefers chunky peanut butter over smooth). This is different than some blatant and unforgivable circumstances.

Safety should never be compromised. Review the recommendations about safety given in Chapter 8. Dating and a relationship should not involve bodily harm or cost a life. Under no circumstance is violence acceptable. Any physical or sexual force is inappropriate at any stage. Any violations require immediate action and reporting. Cell phones can be invaluable. Calling 911 from a fixed pay phone immediately alerts the operator of the location. Even if the caller says nothing, a police officer is usually sent to that location.

Including Indians, no community is immune from abuse and violence. It would be convenient and self-congratulatory to think that such crimes do not occur in the Indian community. Surely, they must be someone else's problem. This myth is rejected by actual numbers. There are shelters and organizations for battered women of Indian origin in the U.S. Created in 1990, Apna Ghar in Chicago has served over 3800 such women of Indian origin, as outlined on their Website. In the San Francisco Bay area, Aasra is similar organization.

Do not do or tolerate anything that contributes to such terrible statistics. Violence should not be a growth industry.

Grounds for Rejection: Deceit

Some bland bending of truth can occur in the context of a relationship. The boy advertised as "athletic" is more of a sports fan than an athlete. The "80% vegetarian" turns out to be 51% vegetarian. This mild misrepresentation is forgivable or negotiable.

Broader deceit is another matter. Claiming to be single while actually married is not acceptable. Both parties should know what each is accepting. It is not acceptable to start another relationship as a back-up to a pending, but concealed engagement. It is not fair to anyone. Notifying someone upfront of children from a previous marriage is different than concealing this information until marriage. Trust is a crucial component of any relationship. Being married to a dishonest person could be misery.

Time Course

Gathering an impression of exactly who is available in the Indian matrimonial process requires some time. It also takes some time to form an impression of what type of spouse one desires. Only experience can allow these thoughts to mature. The novelty of an early experience may allow halfhearted relationship to continue, but the same situation is less tolerable with experience.

My time in residency helped me to clarify my thoughts and determine what kind of traits I would value in a future wife. It also allowed me to detect psychiatric trouble. Accordingly, my tolerance for continuing such a relationship decreased. On one date, a reasonably pleasant varani confessed to me that her weight was much more substantial during college, partly due to late-night gorging. Having ravaged a pizza in the wee hours more than once myself, I did not think much of her confession initially.

Later, I could not help noticing the dainty way that she ate potato chips, holding each chip by the edge cautiously and never allowing them to touch her lips. She then confessed some guilt over eating the "whole snack bag." She decided that consuming potato chips required more rigorous exercise to be added to her already strict schedule.

When she said this, I perceived her to be thinner than I had initially considered, and her cheeks seemed more hollow than before. Perhaps hastily, I detected enough red flags of a possible eating disorder. It would have been totally inappropriate for me to ask about this specifically. After all, I was there on a date, not in session as an evaluating psychiatrist. The twain roles should not meet.

Another time, I thought that a so-so varani would be a fascinating patient. The issues for therapy could have included some conflict over identity, gaps in memory, and her perceptions of her parents. I thought it a pity that I met her socially first, not professionally. Again, never should the two roles meet.

"Farewell," Not "So Long"

The late pianist and entertainer, Victor Borge claimed that, "It is never, 'Good-bye,' but only, 'So long until we meet again.'" Having Danish and Jewish roots, Mr. Borge was most likely never a candidate in the Indian matrimonial process in North America. The fine sentiment of his statement is not always applicable.

Depending on the circumstance of the breakup, continued contact as friends is possible, provided that both are comfortable with this arrangement. Mr. Borge would be correct in this case of "so long," not "good-bye." In other circumstances, the breakup does not favor continued contact. One person may have initiated the breakup, and the other does not agree or approve. Challenging the decision or requesting a continuation may appear like begging or desperation. Even when the breakup is mutual, the aftermath may be unpleasant. In all these cases, it is truly "good-bye."

I went out a couple times with a varani and decided that she was not what I was looking for. I thought that it was "good-bye" and not "so long." She seemed to accept my decision. A few days later, I received a phone call from the varani's father, catching me off guard completely. He asked me how I was doing and exchanged some pleasantries about the weather ("Yes, we could use more rain.") and work ("Yes, it has been a hectic week for me too.").

Mentioning that his daughter seemed upset, he wondered about my reasons and asked if he could do anything to help change my mind. In the course of the discussion, I asked him directly if his daughter actually knew about this call. He admitted that she did not, which unsettled me even more. Somehow the call ended with my having an open invitation to visit them for dinner whenever I am in the area. I have declined the offer thus far.

I did not see the relationship between that varani and me continuing in a friendly way. If I did, I would have continued seeing her. Explaining my specific reasons to her father may have been harmful and certainly not helpful. He essentially went behind her back in calling me in the first place. He may have been well-intentioned, but a bit shady.

My wife once received a call from a varan with an amazing amount of free time. They chatted a few times, and their contact faded away. Some months later, the same guy called her again, much to her surprise. He found it easy to talk with her and wanted a consultation on female point of view. He wondered, for example, if owning real estate increases a man's cachet. Would a convertible help? My wife politely offered some vague answers, but she received no follow-up as to whether her recommendations were helpful or not.

In yet another example, a varani's father returned my dossier with an abrupt and noncommittal note. I moved on and presumably so did she. After more than six months, the varani's father called mine to convey that his daughter thought that I would be a better match for her unmarried cousin in India. Evidently, I was not good enough for the varani herself, but somehow good enough for the Indian cousin. It would nonsense to think that they returned my dossier, because I am too good for the varani, but better suited for her superior cousin.

In all these examples, recontacting someone after a presumably final decision is certainly awkward. Trying to uncover motives for a daughter's breakup is intrusive. Consultation on how to increase one's eligibility can occur with others, not a random varani from some time ago. Trying to impose a relative on an initial reject is inappropriate. Good-bye should be good-bye.

As mentioned earlier, a breakup is different from a "temporary situation" in which one person requires some time away before reconnecting in the future. This would be fine, if both agree.

Means of Breaking-up and Technology

Just as the means of contact have increased, so have the opportunities for delivering bad news. Unsexy means to end relationships include face-to-face contact and a telephone call. More recently, e-mail can serve the same purpose. Sexy celebrities have conveyed their intent by a fax machine and overnight mail. Considering their frequency of divorces, all methods must convey the message effectively.

Means of Breaking-up and the Type of Relationship

Apart from technological advances, how the couple breaks up can reflect their history. After one disastrous date, it may be sufficient to send an e-mail with an official rejection or a message on an answering machine. Relatively casual relationships can end with a phone call. Sending e-mail or leaving a message may be less suitable in a more serious or long-term relationships. Face-to-face contact to deliver news about a breakup is not any easier, but it demonstrates a level of respect to the person and the relationship. It is also less cowardly.

In a breakup, one must consider some practical features such as time, distance, and money. Even if it seems less abrupt to deliver bad news in person, it may not be the best or most practical method. For example, driving a long distance to break up with a more casual relationship may be noble, but not totally necessary.

Inertia versus Courage to Stop

Newton's First Law is that an object at rest stays at rest and an object in motion stays in motion, unless an outside force acts on it. I know plenty of people whose resting inertia is tremendous. Actually, their active inertia is minimal. Maybe I am trying to say that I know plenty of lazy people.

Nevertheless, we can apply the notion of inertia to relationships. Some relationships may be difficult to set into motion. Once in motion, they may continue in motion until influenced by outside forces (e.g., wanderlust, work assignments, meddlesome family, or nuclear war).

An ongoing relationship without clear evidence of progress toward a commitment is usually not tolerated in the Indian community. Nevertheless, a relationship can continue merely because it has existed for some time. It has been in motion. However, a separate question is whether this relationship is compelling. No relationship should continue merely to avoid the pain and messy inconvenience of breaking up. Certainly, it is easy to continue, but it is not fair to either party. By implication, deciding and proceeding to break up requires some courage.

Second Chance

Depending on the circumstances and within reason, some people deserve a second chance. For example, it may have been an isolated event that one person arrived 45 minutes late and appeared totally distracted during the first date. Going out again can help determine if this is typical.

Some other circumstances should not be forgivable. It would be unconscionable to go out again with someone who went away to use the restroom and never returned. It would be torture to go another date if the couple has nothing in common (e.g., couch potato boy who loves all forms of violence with an energetic pacifist girl). Attempting to proceed anyway would be waste of time.

Chapter 15

Engagements and Marriage

"Marriage is the only adventure open to the cowardly."

Voltaire

The previous chapters have described a long journey. First, the boy and girl come into contact through a variety of means. Boy and girl decide to go out. Boy and girl do not find each other disgusting. In fact, each seems fond of the other. As they spend time together, they may increasingly believe that this could become a committed relationship. Moving toward that commitment is a process itself.

Timeframe

With the short timeframe of the Indian matrimonial process, proposals are considered much earlier than in a casual relationship. I was occasionally reminded of this timeframe in talking with my father. The conversation resembled a review with the managed care division of a health insurance company. Both were interested in knowing how many sessions I required to make up my mind to achieve a goal or determine an outcome. In both examples, my estimated timeframe seemed too long. Surely, a more effective suitor or psychiatrist could achieve the same goal in half the time. Authorization for a few sessions was granted, but additional sessions required authorization from the reviewer.

Ready for Marriage

It is worth considering if, in fact, one is ready for marriage. Is this an appropriate time to marry? Is there sufficient maturity to consider married life? Is the person too young and foolish to marry? Alternatively, is the person too old and set in ways to consider the necessary compromises that come with marriage? Is this the natural progression of a solid relationship? Is marriage simply an escape from an unsatisfying situation? If so, are both clear on this purpose?

My friend Kamal once met a varani who gave him the impression that she seemed too happy being single to consider marriage seriously. By contrast, Kamal felt that he was ready for marriage back then. This statement did not demonstrate a desperation or hatred of being single. Rather, he reached a point in his life that he wanted a life-long, committed relationship.

I found Kamal's statement striking at the time. I do not remember my situation exactly, but I myself probably was not "ready" for marriage. I finished the labor known as residency training and had some unique opportunities to travel and work. I do not regret that at all. That interval of time matured me personally. When I met my wife, fortunately both of us were "ready" for marriage.

Proposals: Powerlessness, Commitments, and Ultimata

Concerning the future of any relationship, my wife argues that women retain the most power during the initial phase of courtship. Women can say "yes" to start a relationship or "no" to end one before it starts. Men can accept the decision or attempt to switch the "no" to "yes." Of course, both men and women can end a relationship already underway. However, the ultimate act of proposal still rests on the man's shoulders in the vast majority of circumstances. It would be a liberated and egalitarian circumstance for a woman to propose to a man.

When couples discuss the general possibility of marriage, the woman can hint or plainly state to the varan that she would not mind marrying him. However, it is usually up to the man to follow through. In this way, my wife believes that women are less powerful than in the initial phase.

The related issue is the male side of the equation and the differing ability to commit, as some women commonly complain. Some men do not find commitment too difficult. However, some other men's agonized sense of conflict tortures their female companions. To end the torture, some women may issue an ultimatum: "Propose to me or we are finished." The ultimatum may even come from her parents. Immediate attention or a deadline may be specified as well.

The ultimatum may be enforced, and a marriage or breakup occurs. Similar to predictions of the world coming to an end, the ultimatum may also come and go with no consequence. The couple continuing in that conflicted state implies that the ultimatum had no "teeth."

Personally, I find it sad that any such ultimatum occurs at all. It saddens me that the progression or status of the relationship is not mutually satisfactory. In an old-fashioned way, the continued sense of conflict also puzzles me. After being in a relationship for a long time, what has one person not discovered about the other? Why is official commitment difficult? I am also troubled by the force of the ultimatum: decide or else. In my opinion, it does not signal a solid relationship in the future.

When You Know...

Women pregnant for the first time receive the advice that they will definitely know when they are in labor. The process is not mild. Similar advice applies to worthwhile relationships. Having pleasant sentiments in a relationship is different than feeling that "this is it." The relationship should feel comfortable and compliment both people. If the relationship is worthwhile, expressed and unexpressed feelings declare themselves spontaneously. One person should not feel obligated into feelings that do not truly exist.

Proposals: Gentleman-like Behavior and Protocol

In the past, the boy in the West approached the girl's father to ask for her hand in marriage. That preliminary contact was appropriate and chivalrous, as the marriage required parental approval to proceed. In the best circumstance, the parents heartily approved, and everyone was delighted. If they did not approve, the engagement could not proceed, or the couple married without the parents' blessings—in debtors' prison, if necessary.

Even in recent times, future sons-in-law have continued the practice of contacting the prospective parents-in-law before proposing. Less than asking permission, he is essentially notifying her parents of his plans. Again, in the best circumstance, her parents are pleased to hear the news. Their disapproval may have similar consequences as before.

Historically in India, parents arranged the marriage between boy and girl, eliminating the need for a true proposal between the couple. In a modified circumstance more recently, the boy in India may not propose to the girl directly. Instead, he may relay the proposal to the girl's parents who ideally would discuss this with their daughter. The circumstances are different in an Indian "love marriage" in which the boy and girl eventually disclose their relationship and a likely intent to marry.

The Indian situation in the U.S. is unique. Commonly, the Indian parents themselves had an arranged marriage, or they are certainly familiar with the historical custom in India. They realize that it would be very uncommon for the couple raised in the U.S. to meet each other only at the wedding itself. Similarly, it would be uncommon for a proposal to consist only of a parent notifying the daughter that the boy wants to marry her.

Well before marriage, I once discussed all of these mechanics with my parents. My father identified some possible historical value to the preliminary step of the boy contacting the girl's parents. In this age, however, he dismissed this as an outdated ploy for the boy to win some favors with his potential parents-in-law.

In my case, I proposed to my wife directly. My parents and sister knew about the plan, but no one else. In considering this issue later, my wife was grateful that I did not inform her parents before the proposal. She was not confident that her father would keep the news to himself or would have acted strangely until I proposed. Indeed, I thought that he was going to leap through the telephone with delight when my wife called them to announce our engagement.

Boy's Perspective versus Girl's in Proposal

If the relationship has reached a point of possible engagement, some stability and certainty should exist in the relationship. Instability and uncertainty in relationships keeps me in business, but that is another story. A proposal should occur on some foundation, even in brief courtships. The boy and girl should have a generally good "gut" sense about the other.

As a boy is considering proposing, he should have some confidence that she will say "yes." He should not be guessing at her answer and believe that the odds are not much better than 50/50. Similarly, she should have confidence in her answer and not require a long, weighty time to consider the proposal. In the happiest of circumstances, the boy has predicted accurately, and the girl has confidently accepted.

If there is uncertainty in any of these matters, something is wrong. Someone has misread the situation, or someone is conflicted in some manner. Once again, the question is if the problem rests with one person, the other person, or in the relationship.

Rings and Other Symbols

Depending on the region in India and caste, the symbols of marriage are displayed in some ways. For example, married Brahman men wear two sacred threads of three-strands each. Married South Indian Brahman women wear silver toe rings and a gold necklace with religious coins. These symbols are not as obvious as a Western wedding band or an engagement ring.

Each person's observance or interest in these symbols can vary. Having some Indian symbols may strike some people as overly traditional. This may seem out of place if tradition is not observed on other counts. Having some Western insignia may seem out of place as well. Some symbols may be of greater interest than others.

As the general topic of engagement and marriage surfaces, it is worthwhile to gather a general sense of interest in these symbols. Some varanis may like a Western-style engagement ring. Purchasing an engagement ring after the proposal allows the future bride to participate in the selection.

Angle for Proposal

Just as a boy is considering proposing, he should also consider exactly how to do so. This consideration requires some thought, preparation, and creativity. Various stories abound about specific proposals. Some can be novel and thoughtful. For example, one friend of mine proposed to his then-girlfriend in a helicopter. The brilliance of that plan impressed me. The low oxygen at the high altitude would affect her judgment to his favor. She had no means of escape, and an unsatisfactory answer could have deadly and immediate consequences. Of course, she said "yes." She had no choice, really. Fortunately, they remain happily married.

Other proposals are not intimate. Increasing the scrutiny or pressure of the moment, some proposals have occurred in group settings. The added presence may promote the girl answering "yes," but I also know of a tactless boy who broke an engagement in that setting. That certainly intensified her humiliation and pain.

If we believe them as legitimate, proposals have even occurred on talk shows. Surely, the bent knee imparts some credibility. Nevertheless, it is not exactly personal to propose while millions of viewers watch at home. For that matter, response to the proposal may cause the crowd to chant, "Jerry! Jerry!"

Whether it is a helicopter ride or the Jerry Springer show, the proposal itself requires some thought and planning. The proposal need not be extravagant or larger than life. However, the act should be sincere and thoughtful.

Interval between Engagement and Marriage

This interval can be determined by a variety of factors such as the following: vacation and travel schedules, money, and family concerns. The interval is commonly greater than a year in the U.S., but only a few weeks or months in India.

My wife and I married only two and half months after I proposed. As one of the characters in *When Harry Met Sally* (1989) declares, "When you have decided that you want to spend the rest of your life with someone, you want the rest of your life to start as soon as possible." Another way of looking at this is that I wanted to marry before she came to her senses and changed her mind.

Due to constraints in my then-fiancée's schedule, we married during her vacation. The short interval of time intensified an already hectic process. Given all the planning, telephone calls, e-mail, and faxes, we felt that we had activated a machine that was continually gaining intense momentum.

Despite all the intensity, my wife and I do not regret it. Having only a fixed amount of time decreased the chance of deliberating over less-than-monumental matters (e.g., tapered versus straight candles or the color of napkins at the reception). Also, there were fewer possibilities for our wedding site and receptions. Either the reception hall was or was not available on the date that we wanted.

Engagement Ceremonies

Prior to Hindu weddings, there is an actual engagement ceremony known as *nitshchyathanbulam* in Tamil. A priest conducts this event with both families present. An auspicious time for the marriage is also determined. In yesteryear, this ceremony was very close to the wedding itself. More recently, a longer amount of time can separate the interval between the engagement and the wedding.

An engagement ceremony provides a formality to the relationship and increases the commitment. Being boyfriend and girlfriend is different than fiancé and fiancée. An engagement may be bound verbally or represented by a symbol such as an engagement ring. However, this engagement does not equal one formalized in a religious ceremony, in the opinion of most Indian parents.

In the evolution of a relationship, an engagement ceremony may be a natural development. As implied, parents may be interested in the engagement ceremony to increase the respectability and formality of the engagement. Moreover, breaking an engagement after such a ceremony carries more weight and should be more difficult for both parties. Restless parents may find that difficulty reassuring. In fact, the parents' interests in these matters may be greater than the couple's. If so, the couple may want to determine if they themselves are sincerely proceeding with the event.

I know one example in which the boy and girl began dating seriously while living some distance away from their common hometown. Both sets of parents found it unseemly that these two were happily carrying on. A corrective engagement ceremony ensued, and their marriage followed some months later. Fortunately, the engagement did not force the issue and simply formalized relationship already heading toward a commitment.

Alternatively, an engagement ceremony may be desired to help intensify a luke-warm relationship. Indeed, it may serve that purpose, but this is perhaps a less justifiable reason. The engagement ceremony cannot create something from nothing. It will not automatically change how each person feels about the other, even if the stakes are higher. This also does not totally prevent a breakup.

In another example, I know about an engagement ceremony arranged rather quickly after boy met girl. Without being thrilled with each other, neither strongly objected to the event. The boy and girl seemed to be of marriageable age, and they found each other's company pleasant enough. No general timeframe for a wedding was planned, and this state of limbo continued. From neglect, the couple mutually agreed to end the engagement some time later.

The main difficulty in this situation is that the engagement ceremony was not taken seriously or as a natural outgrowth of a relationship. It was primarily at the parents' command. The sense was that the relationship would fall into place after the engagement ceremony. Indeed, that may have been possible in the appropriate circumstances. Instead, disintegration occurred. The engagement ceremony did not shelter the couple from this outcome.

Location of Wedding: U.S. versus India

Traditionally in India, the wedding is held in the bride's hometown or ancestral village. Deciding the location of the wedding is not so simple with U.S.-raised couples. One possibility is to hold the wedding where the bride grew up in the U.S. A wedding in the U.S. is easier in some ways. Planning domestic travel is not as complicated. Friends and family in the U.S. can attend more easily. Depending on the arrangements, the cost may be lower as well.

The hometown may have general facilities to have a religious ceremony, if one is desired. There may be a preference to have the wedding in an actual place of worship, but this may not be near some Hindu couples. Thus, the wedding may occur elsewhere to satisfy this wish. Priests or others conducting a wedding can travel to the wedding site. I have attended Hindu weddings in reception halls of hotels, large restaurants, and banquet halls. Fortunately for all of us and the fire department, the *agni* (holy fire) was well contained.

There are pros and cons to a wedding in India. Most likely, the couple has elderly relatives and extended family in India. A wedding in India would be more authentic. Any last-minute Indian accessories at the wedding can be more easily purchased. The *nadaswaram* (long pipe) and *mridangam* (drum) players required at any South Indian Hindu wedding are physically present in full force. In the U.S., playing a cassette or CD is just not the same as the musicians' commanding presence and deafening volume. A wedding in India requires increased expense and coordination. Family and friends in the U.S. may not attend.

A compromise is to have a wedding in India and a reception in the U.S. Of course, this adds to the overall expenses, but it combines the best of both approaches.

Invitations: Wording

In Indian wedding invitations of yesteryear, the first-born male of the entire family as the patriarch did the inviting to the wedding. In that capacity, my father-in-law has invited people to several weddings that he himself did not attend. Titles and places of employment were included on invitations. The couple would then be listed with their parents' names as an addendum (e.g., "Karthik, son of Hariharan and Parvathi with Sujatha daughter of Natarajan and Saroja"). Traditional wedding invitations also included a list of those offering their "best compliments." Even if relatives were not entirely respectable, appearing on an invitation made them respectable and important in the moment.

More recently, the traditional format of Indian invitations has been modified. Removing the patriarch's name, the two sets of parents are more often listed as the inviters. Titles, degrees, and the names of employers are not uncommon. This can demonstrate George Bernard Shaw's observation: "Titles are for the mediocre. The truly great are embarrassed by them."

In invitations and other matters related to the wedding, considering equality is worthwhile. Listing only one set of parents on the invitation appears imbalanced and rude. Even if one person's professional qualifications drastically outclass the other's, the difference need not appear on the invitation.

Both sets of parents and the couple should decide on the presentation and the text of the invitation. Ideally, everyone agrees on the one wording that goes to press. After submission, the proof should be examined closely. Correcting any errors on a proof is easier and cleaner. I have seen wedding invitations containing a misspelled name, wrong street address, or incorrect phone number. Including a sheet of "errata" and corrections is tempting, and manually correcting each invitation is tedious and in poor taste.

Printers of Invitations

Obviously, an American printer in the U.S. can print Western-style invitations. Listed in any telephone directory, local printers or card shops usually have a range of simple to fancy wedding invitations. Additionally, many invitations are available at competitive prices over the Internet.

Alternatively, the couple may prefer an Indian-style wedding invitation, whether it uses Indian paper, fonts, or icons. Stationery and printing services are available at Indian stores throughout the country. Even if they are not available at the store directly, often those store owners can make referrals (e.g., "My cousin's brother-in-law used to live next door to a chap who once shared a taxi with a desi whose daughter's accountant knows is a printer.").

In this computer age, genuine Indian invitations are available through the Internet. Printed in the U.S., these can cost less than a non-Indian printer. Rather than endorsing particular Websites, I recommend entering "Indian wedding invitation" on any search engine to learn more about such services.

Yet another option is available. For our wedding invitation, we could not find on the Internet the style from our ancestral region of India. Accordingly, we took advantage of the global village. Some of my then-fiancée's relatives in India went to a few printers and faxed us a few selected fonts for our review. We sent an e-mail with our selection and the text of the invitation. After a rapid turnaround time with the printer in India, the invitations were sent by courier mail to my address in the U.S. Although this process may appear complicated, we were very satisfied with the ultimate result. Moreover, all of this actually cost less than any printing in the U.S.

Apart from standard paper invitations in the mail, one option is to send an invitation through the Internet as an e-greeting. I know one couple who did this. It is cheap and efficient and requires all guests to be cyber-connected. However, it is not a particularly elegant way to invite people to a wedding.

The Guest List

Exclusion at any age can be painful. Children do not like being excluded from play. Being rejected at a high school dance also hurts. Blacks in South Africa were not pleased with apartheid as a policy of exclusion. George W. Bush did not appreciate his exclusion from the Presidency and went to court for inclusion. Consider the length of the chapter on rejections in this book.

Exclusion from a guest list at a wedding is essentially no different. Determining whom to invite should be obvious in some cases. However, it is difficult to know where to draw the line.

Indians often cast a wide net with the guest list. My father recalls personally handing to a whole set of new colleagues invitations to his wedding. He did not know them that well, and his marriage was in a completely different part of the country. Nevertheless, all were invited, although none attended.

I also happened to start a new job when I had become engaged. However, I did not repeat my father's example. Lesser examples of that phenomenon did occur. Before my wedding, my father met a relative of an old friend of his. After mentioning my upcoming wedding, my mother wound up giving an invitation to that relative and the guy who happened to be with him at the time. Neither attended the wedding, nor did we expect them.

The spirit of the vast Indian distribution is like making an announcement rather than providing an actual invitation. All may know that the random and recently invited guest is unlikely to attend. The invited guest may also realize that the invitation is essentially a formality, and attendance is neither required nor expected.

Perhaps in that spirit, I was invited to the weddings of two former varanis. In fact, my whole family was invited. I found it odd and more puzzling than my parents did. I doubt I was truly expected to attend these weddings, and I felt no such obligation.

Chapter 16

Summary and Conclusions

"We shall not cease from exploration and the end of all our exploring will be to arrive where we started…and know the place for the first time."

T. S. Eliot

There is a distinction between a religion and its culture. The former is more structured and ritualized. The religiously observant may pray at fixed times with a set frequency and proscribed manner. By contrast, the culture of a religion encompasses more than the standard rituals of the religion itself. In a more diffuse way, the culture of a religion can refer to a way of thinking and living, not only observances. Upon converting to any religion, acquiring the new observances is easier than becoming familiar with broader qualities of that religion's culture. Religion governs behavior and practice, and the culture of religion can influence thoughts and attitudes.

The distinction between religion and its culture is one way to consider the Indian matrimonial process. The generation of Indians who grew up in the U.S. is usually familiar with the classically arranged marriages in India, because they have encountered stories and living products of that system. That classical approach has been another cultural feature, which is no different than the notion of an extended family.

Religions in India may differ, but the Indian culture at large has a powerful and wide influence. Indian parents of all religions have considered a basically similar method and structure in arranging their offspring's marriage. Such considerations include religion, background, and communal issues such as subcaste. These qualifications have often been spelled out. Once these qualifications of a potential mate have been satisfied, social conventions with less structure begin, as the interested parties actually come together. If a potential alliance proceeds satisfactorily, the engagement and marriage are the next phase of structured rituals. Widespread familiarity with all of these conventions allows everyone a general sense of how to proceed and what to expect.

In India historically, the general protocol with these social customs has been universally known. These obvious and well-recognized conventions would have practically eliminated the need for a "how to" book on traditional marriages in India. If necessary, the more experienced generation could offer its wisdom to the younger group, even if that wisdom were not entirely welcome.

In the 1970s and early 1980s, marriages in the Indian community in the U.S. were not common. Since then, my generation of U.S.-raised Indians has entered marriageable age, but the matrimonial process was not well charted. Those who explored the terrain may have developed some experience, but others may have been more familiar with a different section of the land and another way of exploration. The key difference between the current and the past systems is the absence of clear and well-recognized methods. Some of these methods have been discussed above.

With the disappearance of only one path, the new paths have been less obvious, more numerous, and not necessarily well-marked. The goal of all approaches is the same: a committed relationship from a qualified member of a similar background.

Some approaches represent an Indian format transplanted in the U.S. One such example is meeting as family-to-family prior to the couple dating. Other approaches are uniquely American, as exemplified by mixer parties oriented to the young Indian community. One particular way may have several versions, such as referrals from peers and the peers of parents. As outlined above, the existing range implies that no single approach always works.

Clarity is at the center at the repeated emphasis on thinking about matters for oneself and relaying this clarity to others when applicable. Thinking about the choice of partner should reflect some internal work before any external work. Namely, we must consider what is and is not important to ourselves individually. This consideration applies to personal qualities and cultural matters. Some self-honesty and courage help. As the sense of clarity increases, the remaining task is simply meeting that right person with those qualities. The task is not totally simple, admittedly. However, the preliminary internal work facilitates the external work of finding a mate.

Related to these ideas, my generation of Indians in the U.S. has three cultural influences: purely Indian, purely American, and the Indian community in the U.S. Depending on the circumstance, one aspect or the other may be accentuated, and a mix is inescapable. To be more accurate, a mix *is* escapable, but it was *not* escapable for me personally.

The Indian matrimonial process is not for everyone. There can be some unpleasant encounters with less-than-enthusiastic participants in the process. It is not objectionable to try out the Indian matrimonial process to see if it works for a particular person. However, blatant social indecencies such as rudeness, deception, and wastes of time *are* objectionable. Of course, all of these social indecencies can exist with general human interactions, including general dating. If the desired goal is to marry someone of a similar background, then it may require some faith in two features: the overall system described here and that one will be successful eventually. I myself had some doubts at times, but my faith was eventually rewarded. My story is not an isolated case, and the same ending is available to other couples.

As conveyed, the Indian matrimonial process is deliberate and involves more people other than the would-be couple. The process can be viewed as an unromantic and non-private means to an end. However, there is another way of considering the matter. The Indian matrimonial process is ultimately a mechanism to meet people of a similar background. Some realistic means to reach that goal have been outlined above. Each one of these means has resulted in happily married and well-matched couples.

Regardless of background, the task of finding a suitable mate can be daunting. Some descriptions in previous chapters may not lessen that conviction. However, it can be done. Enough success stories exist for me to feel confident about this statement.

My personal course through the Indian matrimonial process and ultimate marriage were an evolution of thoughts and experiences. And the same is true of my counterparts. Broadly speaking, I felt too "Indian" to marry someone without an Indian connection. At the same time, I felt too "American" to marry someone without that preexisting connection.

Experiencing the Indian matrimonial process or general dating can allow greater learning about one's own personality and lack thereof. Preferences and goals in life become clearer. These features impact one's thoughts about marriage. It then becomes a question of making oneself available for such a relationship to occur.

I thought further about the specific qualities and background of my future wife that would enable us to find our relationship enjoyable, balanced, and enriching. Through perseverance and good fortune, I ultimately married such a woman, and I believe that we have such a relationship. What we have can be certainly replicated by others. Indeed, it has been. Mentioned in the Introduction, my friend Kamal has been happily married a few years now and has marvelous children.

The Indian community has enough fine individuals searching for the same goal for me to believe that there is someone for every interested person. This is a modification of the old observation that there is someone for everyone.

Time and experience can allow us to appreciate Aimé Césaire's observation: "No race has a monopoly on beauty, intelligence, and strength, and there is room for everyone at the convocation of the conquest."

Bibliography

Almeida Costa, J. and Sampaio e Melo, A. *Dicionário de Português* [Portuguese Dictionary] 4th edition. Porto, Portugal: Porto Editora Lda., p. 285.

Ananth, J. and Ananth, K (1996). *East Indian immigrants to the United States, life cycle issues and adjustments.* pp. 21-22. East Meadow, NY: Indo-American Psychiatric Association.

Apte, V. S. (1970). *Student's Sanskrit-English Dictionary* (2nd ed.). New Delhi: Motilal Banarsidass Publishers Private Ltd.

Berry, J. W. (1976). *Human ecology and cognitive styles: Comparative studies in cultural and psychological adaptation.* New York: Sage.

Buss, D. M et al. (1990). International preferences in selecting mates: A Study of 37 cultures. *Journal of Cross-Cultural Psychology, 21,* 5-47.

Buunk, B. P. (1996). Affiliation, attraction, and close relationships. In Hewstone, M., Stroebe, W., and Stephenson, G. M. (eds.). *Introduction to Social Psychology: A European perspective.* pp.346-373. Cambridge, MA: Blackwell Publishers.

Byrne, D. (1971). *Attraction paradigm.* New York: Academic Press.

Chandrasekhar, S. (1984*). From India to America: A Brief History of Immigration and Problems of Discrimination.* La Jolla, CA: Population Survey Review Books.

Cunningham, M. R., Barbee, A. P., and Pike, C. L. (1990). What do women want? Facialmetric assessment of multiple motives in perception of male physical attractiveness. *Journal of Personality and Social Psychology, 59,* 61-72.

Ekblad, S., Kohn, R., and Jansson, B. (1998). Psychological and clinical aspects of immigration and mental health. In S. Okpaku, (ed.) *Clinical methods in transcultural psychiatry.* Washington, DC: American Psychiatric Press.

Erikson, E. H. (1993). *Gandhi's truth.* New York: W. W. Norton.

La Ferla, R. (2002 May 5). Kitsch with a niche: Bollywood chic finds a home. *New York Times,* Section 9, page 1. 5/5/2002.

Mezsaros, A. F. (1961). Types of displace reactions among the post-revolution Hungarian immigrants. *Canadian Psychiatric Association Journal: 6*, 9-19.

Narula, K. C. (2002 June) Indian gays step out. *Little India Publications, 12* (6), 33-45.

News of the Weird (2002 June 21). *Washington City Paper.* P. 6. Citing Kyoto News (2002 April 22).

Saegert, S., Swap, W., Zajonc, R. (1973). Exposure, context and interpersonal attraction. *Journal of Personality and Social Psychology, 25*, 234-242.

Schwartz, J. (1999). *Complete idiot's guide to online dating and relating.* Indianapolis, IN: Alpha Books.

Snyder, M., Tanke, E. D., and Berscheid, E. (1977). Social perception and interpersonal behavior: On the self-fulfilling nature of social stereotypes. *Journal of Personality and Social Psychology, 35*, 656-666.

Thibault, J. W. and Kelly, H. H. (1959). *The Social psychology of groups.* New York: Wiley.

Walster, E., Walster, G. W. and Berscheid, E. (1978). *Equity: Theory and research.* Boston: Allyn and Bacon.

Werner, C. and Parmalee, P. (1979). Similarity of activity preferences among friends: Those who play together stay together. *Social Psychology Quarterly, 42*, 62-66.

Yones, H. (2002). "Chronicle of death foretold." *Harper's Magazine*, January 2004: p.21

Internet Sources

www.a1-dating.com

www.ananova.com/news/story/sm_824151.html

www.cfx.com.au/safety/shtml

www.cyberangels.com

www.hindumatrimonials.com

www.indiandating.com

www.indianlink.com

www.indolink.com/news/international/news_092903_184333.php

www.matrimoniallink.com

www.saferdating.com

www.sage-hearts.com

Appendix 1

Telephone Questionnaire

Name _____ Date _____
Date of Birth _____ Age difference okay _____
Vegetarian? _____ Speaks Tamil? _____
Education/Employment_____
If studying, finish when? _____
U.S.-raised? _____ If not, in U.S. since when? _____
Visa issues? _____
Jathagam match required?
Subcaste a problem? _____
Parents' names _____
Parents' occupations _____
Origins in India _____
Siblings _____
Telephone _____
Address _____
e-mail _____
Exchange dossiers? _____ When will they mail? _____
Notes:
_____
_____
_____
_____

Appendix 2

Alphabeltical List of Indian Matrimonial Websites

www.123india.com/society_and_culture

www.123-matrimonials.com

www.123marriages.com

www.4you.com/im

www.91india.com

www.a1im.com

www.ali.on.ca/islam/matri.htm

www.a1matri.virtualave.net

www.acegift2india.com/ad.htm

www.advertising-in-india.com

www.adsmela.com

www.allbollywood.com

www.allconnection.com/matrimonial

www.angelfire.com/ma/matrimonialindia

www.anuroop.wiwaha.tripod.com

www.appuonline.com/india.directory

www.ashirwad.com

www.asiandating.net

www.asianmatchs.com

www.bareillymart.com/search.html

www.bestindiansites.com/matri1.htm

www.bestmatches.com

www.bridgegroom.com

www.brideorgroom.com

www.busind.com

www.calicutnet.com/otherlinks/matrimon

www.cam-india.com/Matrimonial.htm

www.ceeby.com/matrimonials.cfm

www.chinesematches.net

www.chiranjivirao.com

www.chotabharat.com/matrimonial.asp

www.classifieds.usaindians.com

www.cyberproposal.com

www.daita.com/shaad

www.dialindia.com/society_and_culture

www.delhisingles.com

www.desiempire.com/matrimonial

www.desilink.com

www.detroitindia.com/detroitindia/misc

www.dinamdinam.com/family

www.erols.com/a1action/indc.htm

www.falgunimehta.com

www.findlifepartner.com

www.financialexpress.com

www.findmatch.com/mat/indmat.html

www.gadnet.com/wwwboard/wedding

www.geocities.com/ematrimonials

www.godblessmatrimonials.com

www.godblessmatrimonials.com/kerala

www.hindu.fsnet.co.uk

www.hindumatrimonials.com

www.hindumarriage.com

www.hindustan.net/social/marriage

www.hitecindia.com/deshvidesh/links/su

www.home.earthlink.net/~manish/matri.html

www.hrexchange.com

www.humlog.com

www.humtum.com

www.huntindia.com/matrimonial

www.ib-net.com/links/matri

www.imilap.com

www.in.lycosasia.com/dir/Home_and_Family

www.indnet.org/text.htm

www.indiabook.com/matrimonial/search.html

www.indiainfo.com

www.indialite.com/Matrimonial

www.india-classifieds.com

www.indiaa2z.com/htmlPages/Society_and

www.indiacanadamarriage.com

www.indiafocus.indiainfo.com/society

www.indiagateway.com

www.indialite.com/Matrimonial

www.indiamart.com/khandelwalsabhabarei

www.indiamela.com

www.indian2indian.net/category_pages/

www.indianalliance.com

www.indianlink.com/matri

www.indianmarriages.com

www.indianmarriages.net/main.cfm

www.indianmatches.com

www.indianrishte.com

www.indianWebsites.com/Services/Matrim

www.indian-express.com

www.indiaoptions.com/

www.indiavibes.com/linknet/matrimon.ht

www.indiataj.com

www.indiaworld.co.in/rohini

www.indoaust.com/matr.htm

www.indobride.com

www.indolink.com/Matrim

www.indopak.com

www.infobanc.com/links9.htm

www.infodiary.com

www.jaldikar.com

www.jeevansathi.com

www.kalyanamasthu.com

www.katsi.com

www.link-india.com

www.lookaddress.com

www.lovesites.com/indian.html

www.lovesites.com/International_Sites

www.maayboli.com/dir/Shopping_and_Serv

www.marriage-asia.com

www.marriage.com

www.marriagemaker.com

www.marriageindia.com

www.masalatalk.com/chat.htm

www.matri.com

www.matrimonial.com/IML

www.matrimonial.org/seekcode.htm

www.matrimonial.allindiamart.com

www.matrimonialbank.com

www.matrimoniallink.com

www.matrimonials.achha.com

www.matrimonials.sify.com

www.matrimonialbank.com

www.matrimonialbeginnings.com

www.matrimonialonline.com

www.matrimonials.indianet.org

www.matrimonials.tv

www.matrimonials.usaindians.com

www.matrimonials-india.com

www.matrimonialsindia.com

www.mdnet.co.uk/links/pages/Matrimonial

www.meetmatch.com

www.miabiwi.com

www.milligazette.com/matri.htm

www.mryamrs.com

www.mumbaispace.com/matrimonals.htm

www.myindiatv.com/matrimonial.htm

www.netguruindia.com

www.netwayofindia.com

www.netyourpartner.com

www.nriol.com/classifieds/Matrimonials

www.orinam.com/mimms

www.pyar.org.homepad.com

www.punjabi.net

www.rajputworld.com

www.rishtey.com

www.saagai.com

www.saakshi.com

www.sagaai.com/v2

www.sakeba.com

www.samachar.com

www.sangamamerica.com

www.satna.com/matrimon.htm

www.searchmatrimonial.com

www.searchpartner.com

www.shadi.com

www.sholay.com/Culture/matrimonials.ht

www.shubhlagna.com

www.shubhvivaah.com

www.sikhsamaj.com

www.sikhsingles.com

www.sikhmatrimonials.com

www.sikhseek.com

www.sindh.net

www.singlesindia.com

www.soulkurry.com/v2/relationships/sag

www.southindianmarriage.com

www.southnexus.com/musiclinks.php

www.spiderkerala.com/kerala/matrimonial

www.sreevideos.com/matchmakers

www.subam.com

www.sugandh.com/mommy/matrimonial.html

www.suitablematch.com

www.sumangali.com

www.surfpoint.com/Entertainment_Leisur

www.tamilnet.net.au/tamil_main/matri.h

www.timesmatrimonials.com

www.usaindians.com

www.vadhuvara.com

www.webmarriages.com/charges.htm

www.weddingpros.com/wepics/lata.htm

www.weddingsindia.net/index.asp

Appendix 3

List of Websites Services

Background check
www.checkmate1.com

Collage on Indian marriages
http://www.indiainfo.com/news/2000/05/13/coll

Directory of Indian Websites
www.indianWebsites.com/Services/Matrim

Guide to Indian Matrimonial Websites
www.indiaa2z.com/htmlPages/Society_and

List of Indian matrimonial sites
www.chotabharat.com/matrimonial.asp

Video based
www.sreevideos.com/matchmakers

Appendix 4

List of Websites by Community

Australia

www.indoaust.com/matr.htm

Australian Tamil
www.tamilnet.net.au/tamil_main/matri.html

Bengali

www.miabiwi.com/grooms/ashok.html

Chicago

www.sakeba.com

Christian

www.baicms.com (for born again Christians)

Canada

www.indiacanadamarriage.com

Gujarati

www.falgunimehta.com

Karnataka

www.southnexus.com/musiclinks.php

Kerala

www.spiderkerala.com/kerala/matrimonial
www.pathram.com

Konkani

www.konkani.hypermart.net/india.htm

Marathi
www.maayboli.com/dir/Shopping_and_Serv

Malayali
www.spiderkerala.com/kerala/matrimonia
www.pathram.com

Malayasian Indian Muslims
www.orinam.com/mimms

Non-Resident Indians (NRI)
www.matrimonials.indianet.org
www.nriol.com/classifieds/Matrimonials

South Indians (in India and abroad)
www.southindianmarriage.com
www.bharatmatrimony.com
www.southindianmarriage.com

Punjabi
www.punjabi.net
www.webpunjab.com/indmatrimnl.htm

Rajput
www.rajputworld.com

Sikh
www.sikhmatrimonials.com
www.sikhsingles.com/
www.sikhseek.com
www.sikhsamaj.com

Sindhi
www.sindh.net

Tamil
www.tamilnet.net.au/tamil_main/matri.h
www.kalyanavaibhogam.com/matrilinks

Tamil in Australia
www.tamilnet.net.au/tamil_main/matri.html

Telugu
www.kalyanamasthu.com

United Kingdom
www.netyourpartner.com

U.S.A-specific
www.indiausamarriage.com
www.usaindians.com

0-595-31384-1

www.ingramcontent.com/pod-product-compliance
Lightning Source LLC
Chambersburg PA
CBHW061250280526
45784CB00002B/714